I AM³

THE POWER OF IDENTITY

DONAVON HILL

Trilogy Christian Publishers
A Wholly Owned Subsidiary of Trinity Broadcasting Network
2442 Michelle Drive
Tustin, CA 92780

Copyright © 2020 by Donavon Hill

All scripture texts are from the New King James Version unless otherwise noted. Scripture taken from the New King James Version. Copyright © 1982 by Thomas Nelson, Inc. Used by permission. All rights reserved.

Scripture texts marked NIV® are taken from the New International Version. Copyright © 1973, 1978, 1984, 2011 by Biblica Inc.®. Used by permission. All rights reserved.

Scripture texts marked KJV are taken from the Holy Bible, King James Version. Cambridge Edition: 1769.

All rights reserved, including the right to reproduce this book or portions thereof in any form whatsoever.

For information, address Trilogy Christian Publishing
Rights Department, 2442 Michelle Drive, Tustin, Ca 92780.
Trilogy Christian Publishing/ TBN and colophon are trademarks of Trinity Broadcasting Network.

For information about special discounts for bulk purchases, please contact Trilogy Christian Publishing.

Manufactured in the United States of America

Trilogy Disclaimer: The views and content expressed in this book are those of the author and may not necessarily reflect the views and doctrine of Trilogy Christian Publishing or the Trinity Broadcasting Network.

10 9 8 7 6 5 4 3 2 1

Library of Congress Cataloging-in-Publication Data is available.

ISBN 978-1-64773-072-7 (Print Book)
ISBN 978-1-64773-073-4 (ebook)

To Valerie
love of my life,
wife of my youth,
mother of my children,
grandmother of my grandchildren,
best friend.

Contents

Introduction 7

What Is in a Name 13
The Little Prayer That Changed Everything 25
You Were Made for More 35
Catching a Glimpse 49
The Catalyst 63
Failing Forward 107
Praying Your I Am Statement in the Spirit 117
Remembering the Future 127
Vision Demands Discipline 137
Composing Your I Am Statement 145

Introduction

For years, my friend Greg taught high school in central Louisiana. One day while supervising a group of students who were suffering the misery of after-school detention, he conducted a little experiment. He asked them, "Who is Lil' Boosie?" Greg said they went into great detail explaining to him exactly who Lil' Boosie was. They knew everything about this rap star—his albums, lyrics, girlfriends, kids, birthday, and run-ins with the law. *TMZ* had nothing on these kids.

Then, my wily wise friend, who was also desperately bored at the time, flipped the script. "Now," he asked, "who are *you*?" Greg said you could hear a pin drop. Not a word. Not a peep.

He broke the silence. "You know everything about Lil' Boosie and nothing about *you*!" He continued, "You've spent your valuable time getting to know Lil' Boosie—listening to his music, memorizing his lyrics, reading stories and talking to friends about him, but you don't know *yourself*. Why? Because you've not invested the time and energy required in getting to know yourself."

He pressed in, "What makes *you* tick? Where are *you* coming from? Where are *you* going? What are *your* dreams? What makes you *you*?"

Those kids were blessed that day to hear such wisdom. We would be wise to hear it too.

You and I know a great deal about certain people because we have studied them, be they athletes, musicians, actors, preachers, or whomever. But like those kids in detention, if we were hard-pressed to answer the question, "Who are you?" most of us would have the same blank look on our face. Ask yourself:

Who am I?
What makes me tick?
Where am I coming from?
Where am I going?
What are my dreams?
What makes me me?

And if you are a follower of Jesus, all of this goes even deeper because God has already declared who you are and determined what you are supposed to do. So do you know who *God* says you are? Do you know what *He* wants you to do? Helping you find answers to these questions is the objective of this book.

God deposits dreams deep within each of us. Psalm 37:4 says, *"Delight yourself also in the Lord and He shall give you the desires of your heart."* The word *delight* means "to be pliable." When our hearts are pliable in the hands of the Lord, He puts desires in us, dreams, if you will, that line us up with His will. These dreams are from Him, but they are so fundamental to us, that we consider them to be our own—and indeed they are—because He gave them to us. These dreams are so engrained into our individuality that they come to define us. We become known by them. They are road maps that lead us to our place in His plan. They sync us up to where we fit in to His divine purpose. It is our responsibility to humble ourselves before the Lord, so He can fill us with these desires and dreams. And it is vital that we stay humble before Him, so we can discover and pursue them to the fullest. What He says about us is true, it is reality.

Johanne Wolfgang van Goethe said, "Few men have imagination enough for reality." Let the Word fill your spirit with faith, and God will fill your imagination with Christ-exalting thoughts, ideas, and desires (see 2 Corinthians 10:5). There is a greater reality than just what you see around you. You are not restricted to your current situation or circumstances. As we bow down low to His will and His way, He will help us see that greater reality and raise us up to be who He has said we truly are (see James 4:10 and 1 Peter 5:6). The devil will do everything he can to divert us from the high calling God has for us because he knows, if we ever tap into the power of that calling, hell will suffer heavy losses and heaven will incur heavy gains. We must stubbornly refuse to be distracted by anything less than a life fully surrendered to God.

Mahatma Gandhi said the recipe for finding yourself is to "lose yourself in the service of others." While this is a wonderful concept, there is a missing ingredient. The secret sauce is found in the words of Jesus when He said, "He who finds his life will lose it, and he who loses his life for My sake will find it" (Matt. 10:39). Notice, there is a life to lose before there is one to find. Commenting on these verses, Dr. Timothy Keller points out,

> A disciple is not someone who simply sets a new priority; a disciple finds a new identity. The Greek word that's translated "life" [here] is *psyche*, meaning *self*. [Jesus] is talking pretty radically about the psychological, inner life. "Your

> old way of having an identity, of gaining a sense of self, has got to end. In a sense you have to die to it. And I can give you a whole new identity. You'll [find your] true self." (*The Call to Discipleship*, p. 3, cslewisinstitute.org).

Dying to our old self is the key to finding our new, *true self*. When we are born again, our old self is crucified with Christ and buried with Him, and our new self is raised up by the power of the Holy Ghost (John 3:3–5; 1 Pet. 1:23; Gal. 2:20; Rom. 6:4). This spiritual reality is true to such an extent that Paul told the church at Corinth, "Therefore, if anyone is in Christ, he is a new creation; old things have passed away; behold, all things have become new" (2 Cor. 5:17). Our true self is who God has sovereignly designed and made us to be. Psalm 100:3 says, "Know that the Lord, He is God; it is He who has made us and not we ourselves. We are His people and the sheep of His pasture." Ephesians 2:10 says, "For we are His workmanship, created in Christ Jesus for good works, which God prepared beforehand that we should walk in them." The challenge we face as born-again believers is to continually live from the inside out, *being* our "new, true self," *doing* what God called us to do.

No matter how we feel, what our current circumstances look like or what anybody else says about us, the fact remains: He has designed and made us, we belong to Him, and our lives are filled with glorious purpose. This is not self-centered pride or self-help mumbo-jumbo. This is humility and self-lessness on a grand scale. This is us yielding our will to His and following the example of Jesus, who prayed, "Not my will, but Yours, be done" (Luke 22:42). This is us doing what Paul told the church at Rome to do when he said, "Do not be conformed to this world but be transformed by the renewing of your mind" (Rom. 12:2). Completely surrendering the lower lesser life is the key to finding the higher, abundant life (see John 10:10).

And this surrendered-to-God kind of life is not one that is powerless, weak, and anemic. It is anything *but* that. This kind of life is teeming with power. My friend, Bobby, has a 1971 Chevy Chevelle with a 454 big block 8-cylinder engine, complete with Hooker headers and Cherry Bomb glasspack mufflers. You can hear it coming a mile away. It is loaded with power. And so are you. But what is in you is not muscle car power. It is atomic, nuclear power. It is *who you are at an elemental level.* In the Greek, it is called *dunamis*, which means self-energizing, explosive power.

On December 17, 1938, in Berlin, Germany, Otto Hahn fired a neutron at uranium 235. To his amazement, it split into two lighter elements—barium and krypton. As he interpreted the results of his experiment, Hahn was startled as its implication. He realized that amounts of energy previously thought unattainable and unimaginable were actually within the grasp of humanity. Hahn's discovery quickly sent shockwaves throughout the scientific community. Forty-three days later, the New York Times's headline read, *"Atom Explosion Frees 200,000,000 Volts."* Just like that, the Atomic Age was born and the world has never been the same since. The point is this: the tiniest particles that define the universe and make it what it is—are the source of its greatest power.

This is not a book about atomic or nuclear power, but it is a book about identity. Who you are on the inside, at a spiritually, atomic level, is who you really are. The part of you that makes you *you* is the source of your greatest power. Please do not misunderstand or misquote me. God is the ultimate source of all power, but He has created and called you. He has placed things in you that distinguish and define you. And if you can tap into who you *really* are, your *true* self, then the power of God previously thought to be unattainable and unimaginable becomes available. Ephesians 3:20 tells us that "[God] is able to do exceedingly abundantly above all that we can ask or think according to the power [dunamis] that works in us." Did you catch that? Spiritually speaking, you have 200,000,000 volts inside of you! Heaven is anticipating the day you realize just who you are—and hell is dreading it. The objective of this book is to help you discover and unleash that kind of elemental, spiritually atomic power.

So the answer to the question my friend Greg asked his students years ago, "Who are you?" is simple: "You are who God says you are." Period. The main title of this book, *I Am³*, comes from Exodus 3:14, where God revealed Himself to Moses as "I Am." Because of this, we can declare, "*I am who I Am says I am.*" I have abbreviated the three-peat to, "I Am" with a "3" superscription, which is pronounced mathematically as, "I Am cubed." The artwork is similar to the periodic table of elements because we are who God says we are at an *elemental* level. This book will help you develop your own personal I Am Statement, which, if put into practice, has the power to change your life for good forever.

My prayer is that as you read this book, you are provoked to explore the fullness of who God says you are and to walk in the reality of your true self, advancing the kingdom of God exponentially—and the gates of hell shall not prevail.

What Is in a Name

> And God said to Moses, "I AM WHO I AM."
> And He said, "Thus you shall say to the children of Israel,
> 'I AM has sent me to you.'"
> —Exodus 3:14

A few years ago, our church hosted a pastor's conference for a church consulting company. During the conference, one of the speakers shared some of the difficulties he had faced in his walk with God and how the Lord had proven Himself faithful in those seasons. Then he added this statement: "And now I know Him by *that* Name." I was so moved. I knew exactly what he meant. When he needed comfort, the Lord was his comfort. When he needed strength, the Lord was his strength. "Comfort" and "Strength" are "names" for the Lord, and this guy had called on *that* name in those seasons, and the Lord had come through for him. In this chapter, we are going to explore the idea of His "name."

In the Bible, there are words that refer *to* God, words that we capitalize and call "names," but the truth is, they are not really His Name. From the Hebrew, *Elohim* and *El Shaddai* are two such names. *Yahweh* is another one. Many consider *Yahweh* to be the proper name of God but, in fact, it is not. By pointing this out, I am in no way disrespecting these "names." But if we carefully pay attention to the details here, we will grasp some profound truths.

The name, Yahweh, comes from the Hebrew, *YHWH*, or at least that is how we know it now. The problem is, the name was considered to be so sacred to the Jews that they refused to physically say the word—to pronounce it—for fear that they might "take the name of the Lord their God in vain" and thus violate the command given in Exodus 20:7. They even refused to completely spell it out for the same reason. So they left out the vowels. And even to this day, if you read conservative religious Jewish literature, you will notice when they mention God, they leave out the vowel. In English, they write it like this: *G-d*.

So for generations, nobody said or wrote the most formal Old Testament name for God to the point that, eventually, nobody knew *how* to pronounce it or even write it. The four letters presumed to be pronounced "Yahweh," are referred to by scholars as the *Tetragrammaton*. The Latinized version of the *Tetragrammaton* is the word many of us know as *Jehovah*. In most English translations, the *Tetragrammaton* is translated *LORD* in all caps.

From stories throughout the Bible, there are other words that have been coupled with Jehovah that comprise compound names of God. Again, we call them names, but they are not *proper* names. These compound names highlight certain attributes of God. Each of them reveals something unique about His character and help us to better understand a particular facet of His nature, but not one of them is a proper name. Here are seven compound names of God:

1. Jehovah-Jireh which means "the Lord will Provide" (Gen. 22:14).

2. Jehovah-Rapha which means "the Lord our Healer" (Exod. 15:26).
3. Jehovah-Nissi which means "the Lord our Banner" (Exod. 17:15).
4. Jehovah-Shalom which means "the Lord our Peace" (Judg. 6:24).
5. Jehovah-Raah which means "the Lord our Shepherd" (Ps. 23:1).
6. Jehovah-Tsidkenu which means "the Lord our Righteousness" (Jer. 23:6).
7. Jehovah-Shammah which means "the Lord is Present" (Ezek. 48:35).

Each of these tells us *who* God is and *what* God does. They shed light on His identity, on what makes Him tick. They represent who He is at an elemental level. They are part of His personal *I Am Statement*. These compound names of God are not the only "names" that provide this kind of insight. In Isaiah 9:6, the prophet said, *"For unto us a Child is born, unto us a Son is given; and the government will be upon His shoulder. And His name will be called Wonderful, Counselor, Mighty God, Everlasting Father, Prince of Peace."* Again, here we have the mention of His name, but no proper name is revealed, only attributes. The Bible is full of "names" that describe Him and reveal His character and nature. In one sense, the entire Old Testament is God's I Am Statement! After all, He is "the Word made flesh" (see John 1:14)!

Pastor Ray Pritchard preached a sermon entitled, "Jesus Is Everywhere in the Bible." I love the way he puts it:

> In Genesis he's the Seed of the Woman.
> In Exodus he's the Passover Lamb.
> In Leviticus he's the Scapegoat.

In Numbers he's the Serpent lifted up in the Wilderness.
In Deuteronomy he's the Cities of Refuge.
In Joshua he's the Scarlet thread on Rahab's house.
In Judges he's the Perfect Judge.
In Ruth he's the Kinsman Redeemer.
In I Samuel he's the Trusted Prophet.
In 2 Samuel he's the True Son of David.
In 1 Kings he's the Promise Keeper.
In 2 Kings he's the Jealous God.
In 1 Chronicles he's our Reigning King.
In 2 Chronicles he's our Deliverer.
In Ezra he's the Faithful Scribe.
In Nehemiah he's the Rebuilder of Broken Walls.
In Esther he's Mordecai at the Gate.
In Job he's My Redeemer Who Lives Today.
In Psalms he's the Lord who is my Shepherd.
In Proverbs he's our Wisdom.
In Ecclesiastes he's our True Satisfaction.
In Song of Solomon he's the Beautiful Bridegroom.
In Isaiah he's the Suffering Servant.
In Jeremiah he's the Righteous Branch.
In Lamentations he's the Weeping Prophet.
In Ezekiel he's the Son of Man.
In Daniel he's the Fourth Man in the Furnace.
In Hosea he's the Faithful Husband.

In Joel he's the One Who Restores.
In Amos he's the Burden Bearer.
In Obadiah he's the Mighty Judge.
In Jonah he's the Foreign Missionary.
In Micah he's our Peace.
In Nahum he's the Avenger.
In Habakkuk he's the Lord in His Holy Temple.
In Zephaniah he's the Lord Mighty to Save.
In Haggai he's the Lord of Hosts.
In Zechariah he's the Fountain of Cleansing.
In Malachi he's the Sun of Righteousness.
(Keep Believing Ministries, November 9, 2010, keepbelieving.com)

Here are a few other names, some of which reach into the Gospels and Epistles: Father to the prodigal, Peace to the storm, Wholeness to the broken, Comfort to the comfortless, and Power to the powerless. Whatever you are facing, He has a name for that. He is who He says He is, and He will be who you need Him to be, hence, "*I Am that I Am.*" And when you call on His name in that challenging situation, and He takes you come through it, like my friend, you will know Him by *that* name. No wonder Joel 2:32 says, "Whoever calls on the name of the Lord shall be saved." No wonder Proverbs 18:10 says, "The name of the Lord is a strong tower; the righteous run to it and are safe."

All of these are names, yes, but none of them is a proper name for God. The prophet, Zachariah, however, said that a day was coming when a singular name, a proper name, would be revealed. Notice Zachariah 14:9: "*And the Lord shall be King over all the earth. In that day it shall be—'The Lord is one, and His name one.'"* That name would summarize all of the attributes of our great God and Savior. But for four thousand years, nobody knew that name.

And then on one particular day, one particular angel told one particular girl one particular name. When the fullness of time was come, Gabriel was sent to the city of Nazareth to tell a young virgin girl named Mary, *"You will conceive and bear a Son, and you shall call His name Jesus"* (see Galatians 4:4 and Luke 1:31). That was it! That was the name! After four thousand years of men "calling on the name of the Lord" without ever really knowing His name, now they had a name (see Genesis 4:26). With hundreds and hundreds of words describing Him, now all of these descriptions could be summed up in one singular word, a name, *the* name: Jesus!

Up until this time, the name "Jesus" had been a common, ordinary, garden-variety name. But when it was assigned to this specific individual from Nazareth, who also happened to be the Messiah, the Son of Man, the Son of God, the Seed of the Woman, that name became anything *but* common. It became extraordinary, the Name that is higher than any other, the name before which every knee will bow (see Isaiah 45:23, Romans 14:11, Philippians 2:9–11, Revelation 5:13)!

And not only is it a name that has been revealed, it is a name that has been given. Isaiah 9:6 says "a Son is given." John 3:16 says the same thing: "For God so loved the world that He gave His only begotten Son." As the Son has been given, so has His name. Peter said in Acts 4:12, "Nor is there salvation in any other, for there is no other name under heaven *given* among men by which we must be saved."

And when you call on the name of Jesus, you are calling on Jehovah-Jireh, Jehovah-Rapha, Jehovah-Nissi, Jehovah-Raah, Jehovah-Tsidkenu, Jehovah-Shammah. All of His characteristics, attributes, and power are summed up, sealed up, and wrapped up in that holy and matchless name. Our provision, healing, victory, peace, guidance, righteousness, and help are all contained in one "place," and His name is Jesus. All that He is, is in that Name. When God told Moses in Exodus 3:14, "I Am who I Am," He was, saying, "I Am who I Am says I Am!" After all, He is who He says He is, right? This was the ultimate I Am Statement! And since Hebrews 13:8 says He is "the same yesterday, today, and forever," *He still is what He said He was!* He is who He says He is!

Theologians refer to God's aseity, which means His unchanging consistency, His self-sufficiency and self-existence. In Malachi 3:6, He said, "For I am the LORD, I do not change." If our great God was ever a rescuer, healer, deliverer, seeker, saver, shepherd, or anything else, then He still is. And all of who He is is wrapped up in His name: Jesus! When You say, "Jesus," you have just summed up and encapsulated everything He has ever said about Himself. Colossians 2:9–10 says: "For in Him dwells all the fullness of the Godhead bodily; and you are complete in Him, who is the head of all principality and power." His name is filled with power and purpose. In Matthew 28:18–20 when Jesus had risen from the dead, He met with His disciples and told them:

> All authority has been given to Me in heaven and on earth. Go therefore and make disciples of all the nations, baptizing them in the name of the Father and of the Son and of the Holy Spirit

Hebrews 1:3 says that Jesus is "the brightness of [God's] glory and the express image of His person." Again, all that

God is is expressed in Jesus, and when you say His name, you are bringing to bear everything that is in that name.

What About Your Name

When your name is mentioned, what is the significance behind it? My name, *Donavon*, is Irish and means "brown strong warrior." While in the summer, I get brown, and I think I am a strong warrior, that kind of "what does your name mean" is not what I am talking about. In Acts 13, there is the coolest story of "certain prophets and teachers" who were praying and fasting together. Among them were Barnabas and Saul. During the prayer meeting, the Lord said, "Separate unto me Barnabas and Saul to the work for which I have called them" (Acts 13:2). Immediately, Barnabas and Saul boarded a ship and headed for the island of Cypress, which was home for Barnabas. Once there, they were joined by John Mark, Barnabas's cousin, and began to preach the Gospel from one end of the island to the other. While in the town of Salimas, Sergius Paulus, the governor of that Roman senatorial province sent for Barnabas and Saul to hear the Word of the Lord. As he heard their preaching and teaching, faith came because that is how faith comes (see Romans 10:17). The result was Sergius Paulus repented. He began to turn in faith to Jesus. But there was this guy named Elymas or Simon Barjesus, as he is sometimes called, who was a Jewish sorcerer and who attempted to turn Sergius Paulus away from the faith. Elymas was hindering and withstanding "the work" to which Barnabas and Saul had been called. Because of this blatant blasphemous opposition, Saul snapped. Notice verses 9–12:

> Then Saul, who also is called Paul, filled with the Holy Spirit, looked intently at him and said, "O full of all deceit and all fraud, you son of the devil, you enemy of all righteousness, will you not cease perverting the straight ways of the Lord? And now, indeed, the hand of the Lord is upon you, and you shall be blind, not seeing the sun for a time." And immediately a dark mist fell on him, and he went around seeking someone to lead him by the hand. Then the proconsul believed, when he saw what had been done, being astonished at the teaching of the Lord.

Wow! As my grandmother would say, Saul "took the bull by the horns"! He did not let Elymas get away with his subtle mischievous undermining of what God was doing in the heart of Sergius Paulus. After this confrontation, however, Saul was never referred to again as "Saul" with the exception of a few flashback passages. From here on, he is called "Paul." Interestingly, he and Barnabas are never referred to again as "Barnabas and Saul," in that order. From here on, they are always called "Paul and Barnabas." Saul entered this conflict as a "prophet" and "teacher," but from this point on, he self-identifies as *Paul* and refers to himself as an apostle (see Acts 13:1, Romans 1:1, 1 Corinthians 1:1, 2 Corinthians 1:1, Galatians 1:1, Ephesians 1:1, Colossians 1:1, 1 Timothy 1:1, 2 Timothy 1:1, Titus 1:1). In other words, when you said the name "Paul" in reference to *this* guy, there was a calling wrapped up in his name. Who he was at an elemental level was connected to his name. He was a leader, a trailblazer, and a devil defeater.

Incidentally, this was Paul's first recorded miracle in his amazing ministry, and notice, it was a negative one—he made a guy blind! But he had experienced the very same thing, right? Years before, when he had opposed the work of God, Jesus knocked him down on the road to Damascus and struck him blind. Maybe he was thinking, *Well, it worked for me so here goes...* We do not know if Elymas ever came to faith or knew just what—or who—had hit him. But the devil that was manipulating this sorcerer knew exactly what and *who* had hit him. Another story in the Book of Acts shows us this.

In Acts 19, we see the fascinating story about the seven sons of Sceva. Notice verses 13–16:

> Then some of the itinerant Jewish exorcists took it upon themselves to call the name of the Lord Jesus over those who had evil spirit saying, "We exorcise you by the Jesus whom Paul preaches." Also there were seven sons of Sceva, a Jewish chief priest, who did so. And the evil spirit answered and said, "Jesus I know, and Paul I know; but who are you?" Then the man in whom the evil spirit was leaped on them, overpowered them, and prevailed against them, so that they fled out of that house naked and wounded.

Did you catch that? Jesus was known in hell and so was Paul. Their monikers, "Jesus" and "Paul," meant something in that dark realm. All of God's redemptive work was summed up in the name, "Jesus," and all God had called Paul to be and do was summed up in his name, "Paul." When the devil heard the name, "Paul," in reference to this particular guy from Tarsus, he knew he was an apostle called by Jesus. The devil knew this guy had found his place in the redemptive plans of God.

Let me ask you, who are *you?* When the devil hears *your* name, does he know it? Does he know what your calling is? Does he know what you have been put on this earth to do? I would submit that before he can know it, *you* have to know it. Paul's name and calling became apparent as he faithfully walked with the Lord to the best of his ability. "Saul" was the name of Israel's first king. Saul of Tarsus was from the same tribe, the tribe of Benjamin. But "Paul" was a Greek name. Saul would become an apostle to the Gentiles and his name reflected that.

I do not believe we have to change our names to reflect who we are in Christ and what we are called to do. But I do believe that as we live out our I Am Statement, our very names become identified with our calling. God wants us to live so profoundly in the reality of who He says we are that when we hear our own name and when others hear our name, that calling comes to mind.

The Little Prayer That Changed Everything

This above all: To thine own self be true.
—William Shakespeare; *Hamlet*; Act 1, Scene 3

Valerie and I try to get away for a few days every year to refresh and refocus. While on these little getaways, we pray for our marriage, family, finances, business, church, and any needs that may be pressing at the time. We discuss these areas of our life, what the Word of God says about them and what we believe the Lord is speaking to us about them. Then we pray and script a prayer that specifically addresses each of these areas at that particular season.

Every day, during the months following, we pray this prayer, sometimes together, sometimes apart. To say it is a "routine" is demeaning and takes away the life-changing power that has been released through these prayers. It is more accurate to say that this continual focusing and refocusing keeps us on point, in our lane, fresh and ready to seize whatever season of life we are in. It has proven to be a game-changer.

A few years ago, while on one of these little getaways, as we were seeking the Lord, we felt inspired to write a prayer, a confession, if you will, that helped bring more clarity than ever before to just *who* we are and what *we do*. That prayer became the inspiration for this book. While it has evolved somewhat since it was originally written, I have prayed this prayer, or some version of it, every day since that time. Obviously, the pronouns are changed when Valerie and I pray through it together, or when she prays it by herself, but here is the original prayer from 2016.

> I am a successful pastor of a powerful and growing church. I lead with wisdom, excellence, boldness and confidence.
>
> I am a man of tremendous influence. I have favor with God, favor with man, and I am feared in hell.
>
> I plant and water with joy and faith knowing God is giving the increase and I am anxious for nothing.
>
> I am a ridiculous giver. I am known for my generosity and I am a blessing to the Body of Christ worldwide.
>
> Debts are eliminated, reserves are generated. LifePoint is a financial powerhouse with more than enough to do all God has called us to do.
>
> People are looking at us and saying, "Of all people, I never thought it would be you who is so blessed!"

This is the little prayer that changed everything. It literally revolutionized our lives. When times were good, we prayed the prayer. When times were tough, we prayed the prayer. When we felt it, we prayed the prayer. When we did not feel it, we prayed the prayer. When it looked like the prayer was spot-on, we prayed the prayer. When it looked like it was dead wrong, we prayed the prayer. The reason we prayed the prayer "in season and out of season" is because we had set time aside to seek God, and in the sincerity of our hearts, we believed He had spoken to us, and from that day forward, we determined to make our words match what He had said, regardless of our feelings or circumstances (see 2 Timothy 4:2). This prayer was the means to an end. It became the method whereby we could agree and align with what *He* had said about *us*. Remarkably, the more we prayed the prayer, the more convinced we became that we really *are* who He says we are. I call this prayer, our *I Am Statement*. And as we consistently, persistently prayed our I Am Statement, the elemental truths in it began to resonate deep within our core, at an *atomic* level, if you will, empowering us in ways we never imagined.

The Gap

There can be a gap between what God *says* about us and the way we *actually live*. Often, the fullness of what God has promised us, both in His Word and in our hearts, is not fleshed out in our everyday lives. Too many believers are unaware of what God has already said about them, and certainly, the vast majority do not live up to it. He says we *are* one thing, yet more often than not, we live like we are something else. Philosophers and theologians allude to this gap when they refer to truth in three different respects: conceptual, propositional, and incarnational. What He has conceived and proposed for us, we struggle to incarnate. The problem is not in His declaration—it is in our manifestation. I pray this book helps to close that gap. God wants us to boldly walk in the reality of everything He has declared about us.

Right now, say this out loud, "*I am who I Am, says I am.*" Let that resonate in your spirit.

God has a calling on your life. He has declared it over you. He has spoken it generally in His Word and specifically in your spirit. If you are a believer in Jesus, it is encoded into your spiritual DNA. It is who you are at the deepest level, at an atomic level, at your core. It is your higher self, the one you find when you take up your cross and die to your lower self. And, brothers and sisters, it is time for that spiritual DNA to be activated. It is time for that atomic power to be released. It is time for you to awaken to who you are in Christ and walk into your destiny.

If you have never walked in that calling before, then He wants to awaken you to it. Maybe you have walked in that calling before, but for some reason, you backed off. If that is you, then God wants to get you back on track, back into your grace-groove. Paul said in Romans 11:29, *"The gifts and calling of God are without repentance."* Most translations say the gifts and calling of God are *irrevocable*. I like God's Word translation of this verse: *"God never changes His mind when He gives gifts or when He calls someone."*

Perhaps you have been frustrated with the direction your life seems to be going. I am familiar with that frustration. I have dealt with it in my own life, and in over thirty years of ministry, I have seen it in the lives of many others. I have come to believe that most of our frustration is rooted in two facts. (1) We are not fully convinced we are who He says we are. (2) We are too easily influenced by our feelings and circumstances. When His Word is not the ultimate authority for our lives, we will not walk in the fullness of God's calling, and we will experience ongoing frustration.

I AM[3]

The truth is, we will never experience fulfillment, joy, and satisfaction until we are actively and fully engaged in our calling, walking in the Father's will. In Luke 4, Jesus declared to a stunned audience in His hometown just who He was and what He was called to do.

> So He came to Nazareth, where He had been brought up. And as His custom was, He went into the synagogue on the Sabbath day, and stood up to read. And He was handed the book of the prophet Isaiah. And when He had opened the book, He found the place where it was written: "The Spirit of the LORD is upon Me, because He has anointed Me to preach the gospel to the poor; He has sent Me to heal the brokenhearted, to proclaim liberty to the captives and recovery of sight to the blind, to set at liberty those who are oppressed; To proclaim the acceptable year of the LORD." Then He closed the book, and gave it back to the attendant and sat down. And the eyes of all who were in the synagogue were fixed on Him. And He began to say to them, "Today this Scripture is fulfilled in your hearing."

Notice, in verse 17, He opened the book of Isaiah and "found the place where it was written." After He read the verses from Isaiah, He sat down and said, "Today this Scripture is fulfilled in your hearing." In other words, "That's Me!" The man Christ Jesus had found Himself in the Word.

He was saying, "I am Who I am says I am." And it was a shocker to His audience. To them, He was just Joseph's boy, but the Word said He was much more.

In some respects, Jesus is our substitute. He did things for us that we could not do for ourselves. But in other respects, Jesus is our example. He did things so we could follow after Him and do the same things. In Luke 4 Jesus exampled three powerful truths. 1. He found Himself in the Word. In other words, He found Who He was at His core, His calling, and destiny. 2. He declared what the Word said about Him. He stood up and made it plain. 3. He fleshed it out. He was obedient, submissive, surrendered. And as He walked in the Father's will, He experienced fulfillment that can come from no other source.

In John 4:34, Jesus said to His disciples, "My meat [satisfaction] is to do the will of my Father." There is something so satisfying about walking in the Father's will. Incidentally, His submission to the Father pleased the Father, too. Earlier, Jesus had insisted that John the Baptist water-baptize Him in order "to fulfill all righteousness" (which means to fulfill the will of the Father). As He emerged from the water, the Father declared, "This is my beloved Son, in whom I am well pleased" (see Matthew 3:13–17). There is a reciprocal satisfaction and pleasure that results from our aligning with the will of the Father.

Say that again, *"I am who I Am says I am!"* Let that flood your soul.

In 1943, Abraham Maslow proposed his theory of the hierarchy of needs. Maslow identified the top tier of human achievement as "self-actualization." I believe true self-actualization, and the subsequent peace and fulfillment that accompanies it, only comes from finding yourself in the Word and walking in your calling. You can see this universal quest for a higher life in world religions. Buddhists speak of *nirvana* while Hindus aspire to *moksha* and Muslims seek *jannah*. While these perspectives are distortions of the fundamental teachings of the Christian Bible, I believe they are indicative of a primal hunger within humanity, and a search for satisfaction that can only be found in fellowship with the Father, and fulfillment that is only found in doing His will. I believe they represent the universal quest for the higher self, the abundant life that Jesus referred to in Matthew 10:39 and John 10:10.

Let me warn you, the hardest thing you will ever do is *believe* that you are who He says you are. And the next hardest thing you will ever do is *live* like you believe it. The truth is we have less of a problem believing God is Who He says He is than we do believing we are who God says we are. For instance, we say things like "God is great! He is the Creator of heaven and earth!" Yet we only know these things about Him because *He told us in His Word*. We say Jesus died for us and rose from the dead, but we only know these gospel facts because *He told us so in His Word*! But then, strangely enough, we turn right around and say, "I'm a nobody," "God could never do anything for someone like me," "I don't deserve anything from God," "Bad things always happen to me," "Doors never open for me," and "I always miss opportunities." These things do not line up with what God has said about us, but they may represent how we *feel* or the way things *look* at the time.

We are quite adept in quoting a Bible verse like, "All have sinned and fallen short of the glory of God" (Rom. 3:23), and we often feel like the paragon of virtue and humility for admitting it. But the truth is that verse is not the Father's *final* word. There is more in the book than *bad* news. The big story in the Bible is the *good* news. That means there is more to what the Great I Am has said about us than we "have sinned and fallen short." Brothers and sisters, we have been born again, called out of darkness into His marvelous light, made to be the righteousness of God in Christ Jesus (see John 3:5, 1 Peter 2:9, 2 Corinthians 5:21). And check this out, we know all of this because He said so in His Word. Again, we know who He is and we know He has made us to be because of the same reason—*He told us so in His Word!* The same Word that tells us Who God is tells us who we are. He said it and that settles it. His Word is the foundation of our faith.

When we say things about ourselves that differ from God's final Word, things that do not include the rest of the story of what He has said about us, then we are telling a half-truth at best or calling God a liar at worst. And there is nothing humble about that. As a matter of fact, that is the epitome of arrogance. When we say things about God that are contrary to His Word, it is considered heresy, false doctrine, or even blasphemy. But it is the same when we say things about ourselves that are contrary to His Word.

I was raised in church and loved the Lord from a very early age. I was a young wannabe preacher. In my late teens, through an awful series of events, I became disillusioned and walked away from the Lord. I swore I would never go back to church and I did not even know if God was real. I was dechurched. It was tragic. But then, a few years later, in ways I could never have imagined, Jesus rescued me. And as I began to walk with Him again, I started seeing in the Word just Who He is, how wonderful He is, how powerful He is, how truly good He is. And I also began to get an understanding, a revelation, if you will, from the Word as to just who I am in Him, who He has called me to be, and the power and authority in which I am to live my life.

I AM[3]

And quite frankly, as I began to see this, I was humbled, empowered, emboldened, delighted, and overwhelmed by His amazing grace. During this time of discovery, while I was ministering in southern California, a good friend of mine called me. He and I had walked away from the Lord at around the same time. We had been rebels together and vehemently opposed to church, the Lord, the Bible, and pretty much all things Christian. He and I were fiercely committed to never have anything to do with the church again. And here I was, just a few years later, right back in the middle of it. And not only that, I was a preacher. And while I had come back, my friend was still very much a prodigal.

In our phone conversation that night from my hotel room in San Diego, I began to tell my friend about the miracle of me coming back to the Lord and how I had discovered that so much of my view of God had been distorted and skewed. I explained to him that, somehow, I had gotten the wrong impression of Jesus. I told him that now I was just beginning to see how good God really is; that He is *for* us, not against us; that He has called us to live a life of victory and freedom; that the Cross is the means to a powerful end; that the empty tomb is a testimony to His cosmic victory; that the ascended Savior ever lives to make intercession for us; and that we have been called into a holy, covenant relationship with Him. As I was sharing my heart with my friend, he got very quiet. Then, with an intensity in his voice, and a vitriol that only bitterness can produce, he proceeded to mercilessly berate me. With one final blow, he said, "You are so arrogant! Who in the world do you think you are?"

Although my heart was heavy for my friend and tears welled up in my eyes, my reply was one of quiet resolve. I said, "I am who I Am, says I am."

Now, we may not always feel like we are who He says we are (I certainly did not feel it in my hotel room that night), but our feelings have nothing to do with the truth of God's Word. We would do better if we allowed our feelings to be the caboose and our faith to be the engine. When we put our feelings ahead of our faith, we are sure to derail. That is a train wreck waiting to happen. *The truth is our feelings and our experiences neither validate nor invalidate the Word.* The Word stands alone. Throughout this book, I am going to share concepts that, if you will apply them, they will help you discover and confidently walk in the reality of who God says He is and who God says you are. I am convinced that you, the *real you*—the *one and only you*, the you *God* has created you to be, the you the devil is *afraid* of *you* becoming—is about to awaken and emerge, advance and fulfill your God-given destiny, and that, because of *you*, the world will never be the same. One of the greatest biblical examples of someone who found himself in the Word and began to pray a personal "I Am Statement" is none other than the father of the faithful, Abraham.

You Were Made for More

> *"It is winter in Narnia," said Mr. Tumnus, "and has been for ever so long...always winter, but never Christmas."*
> —C. S. Lewis, Chronicles of Narnia

The story of Abram begins right after the flood. God had instructed Noah and his descendants to multiply and migrate throughout earth. They multiplied all right, but instead of spreading across the face of the earth, they gathered together in one central location—the valley of Shinar. Then, under the direction of Nimrod, a spiritual outlaw and the world's first global dictator, they constructed the infamous Tower of Babel. It was an enormous undertaking that testified both to the brilliance of human ingenuity and the depravity of the human soul. The Tower of Babel was the centerpiece of a false religious system, designed by man, to save himself. It was the beginning of postdiluvian institutionalized false religion. However, in trying to save himself, man lost both God and himself.

Rabbinical tradition says the religion of Nimrod taught that the God of Noah, Shem, Ham, and Japheth was precocious at best and evil at worst. Either way, they thought He was bad and that humanity should seek out other gods to worship and petition for help and protection. Abraham's family worshiped these false gods and, actually, physically manufactured idols which were used to adore and venerate them.

From Adam to Noah, there were ten generations encompassing one thousand years. During this time, humanity quickly and dramatically lost his way, so much so, that God had to flood the earth to reboot His plan. Then, from Noah to Terah, Abram's dad, there were ten generations and only four hundred years. One reason why *these* ten generations took less time than the previous ten is because people were only living about half as long—just a mere four hundred years or so. However, it was still plenty enough time for humanity to completely derail. We see this particularly in Abram's neck of the woods, Babylonian Ur.

By the time of Abram, he and his people believed in many gods—a pantheon of gods—and they believed their religious system was the gateway to these gods. *Babylon* can mean "the gate of the gods." It was crazy and "confusing," which is another meaning of the word *Babylon*. Abram's world was baffling, filled with man-made gods and perverse religious ideations. The bottom line is this, Abram and his ancestors worshiped false gods. Joshua 24:2 confirms this when it says, *"Long ago your forefathers, including Terah the father of Abraham and Nahor, lived beyond the river and worshiped other gods."*

Years later, when Abram's grandson, Jacob, married a girl named Rachel, we see Babylon's influence on her life. She stole her father's "household gods"—that's Babylon (Gen. 31:32–35; 35:2–4). Archaeology shows that Ur was a center for moon worship. Even the names surrounding the story of Abram reflect the influence of the moon god, including Terah, Laban, Sarah, and Milcah. Dr. Ralph F. Wilson points out the predominate gods in Abram's world.

I AM[3]

Abram's ancestors had four leading deities: An, Enlil, Enki and Ninhursag. And they had three chief astral deities: Nanna (the moon), Nanna's son Utu (the sun) and Nanna's daughter Inanna. Nanna, the moon-god, was the main deity of Ur and was represented by the crescent moon. Abram's people worshiped in temples as well as ziggurats with small temples on the top. These temples were staffed by priests, who offered sacrifices, as well as singers and musicians.

Included in the worship of these false gods and goddesses were the practices of child sacrifice, perverse sexualized ritual, and of course, straight-up idolatry. While not identical, the underlying religious presumptions espoused by Abram's generation thousands of years ago are still with us in the twenty-first century. The book of Revelation suggests that these very ideas, from Abram's time, will be around during the time of the Antichrist and his world-dominating religious system, which is referred to as Mystery Babylon (Rev. 17:5).

Interestingly, *Terah* means "inspired," which seems to indicate that Abram's father was an inspirational and charismatic character. He was a promoter of sorts, an evangelist who propagated the message of Babylon. And with certainty and zeal, he passed the message of Babylon and Nimrod down to his children, including his son, Abram. There was a rottenness that went generations deep in this family, and Abram was destined to be the next in line. He would inherit it all, take his place as the patriarch, and lead the family and the rest of the world deeper into the abyss of Babylonian darkness, except for the fact that God had another plan. When

Abram was seventy-five years old, God interrupted the passing of this religious baton from Terah to Abram. Think about that. Seventy-five years into his journey, the Lord broke into Abram's world to tell him, "*You were made for more!*"

Changing Seasons

If we are honest, many of us, like Abram, come from a bunch of messed-up folks, too. And some of our backgrounds are just as baffling as Babylon. Our lives are built on the influence of the previous generations, which can be good, but is often not-so-good. Like layers of earthen strata, often we find ourselves atop of heap of moral, mental, and religious chaos. With the best of intentions, and while totally oblivious to truth, our families can be as enthusiastic about us living out "the family dream" as Terah was about Abram following in his footsteps. I would dare to say that there are some in your family who are convinced that it is impossible for you to "do life" any differently than they did. As harsh as this may sound, they are expecting you to bow at the same altars to the same gods, live with the same traditions and suffer with the same addictions, brokenness and struggles. They love you, but they expect you to embrace their same twisted view of God and His goodness and then turn around and pass it down to your kids and grandkids. In other words, they plan for you, your kids, and your grandkids to live the same low life they have lived—directionless, clueless and detached from the plans and purposes of God. But I believe God has called you just like He called Abram. He is saying to you, "*Hey, ten generations of ordinary is enough! This eleventh generation will be different! I'm calling you to the extraordinary! You were made for more!*"

In Israel, as generations built on the ruins of previous generations, mounds were formed. These artificial hills are called "tels." They are mounds of accumulated ruins, and you can find them all over Israel. Sometimes our lives, too, are built on the mounds of accumulated ruins. But the past does not have to dictate the future. The most well-known tel in Israel is Tel Aviv, Israel's second largest city. In Hebrew, "Tel Aviv" literally means, "ruins spring." It connotes the idea: "from ruins comes renewal." God intercepted the transmission of values from Terah to Abram, thus disrupting the enemy's plans for Abram and his family. The moment Abram began listening to the Voice was the moment his season changed. And from the wintery ruins of Babylon, came the springtime of redemption. And I believe the Voice is speaking to you and me too. Say these words out loud: *"My season has changed."*

In Joshua 7, we have the record of the devastating story of Achan. When the children of Israel miraculously took Jericho, the first city in the Promised Land, they were instructed to not take any of the spoils individually because it all belonged to the Lord. Jericho was a tithe of the Promised Land, the firstfruits of their increase. And yet, Achan stole a beautiful Babylonian garment, two-hundred-and-fifty pieces of silver and a bar of gold from Jericho. The results were tragic. As Israel attempted to take Ai, the next city, they were abruptly rebuffed and thirty-six Hebrews lost their lives. Joshua sought the Lord, and it was soon revealed that Achan was to blame. He and his family, along with their possessions and even their animals, were all stoned to death and burned in the Valley of Achor, which literally means the "Valley of Trouble." But in Hosea 2:15, the Lord says He would transform the Valley of Achor into a door of hope, lush with vineyards and life. Isaiah 65:10 says the Lord would make this same valley a place where herds and flocks would feed and lie down. God knows how to bring hope out of trouble. God knows how to bring life out of death. The empty tomb of Jesus attests to that.

Jesus said, "*He who finds his life will lose it, and he who loses his life for My sake will find it*" (Matt. 16:29). In this passage, New Testament scholar, Kenneth Wuest, refers to the life that Jesus said we are supposed to *lose* as the "low life," and the life we are supposed to *find* as the "high life" (*Word Studies in the New Testament Greek*, Kenneth Wuest). There is a low life we must lose and a high life we must find. This high life is a place of blessing, favor, abundance, and freedom. Philippians 3:14 says, "*I press toward the mark for the prize of the high calling of God in Christ Jesus.*" In Isaiah 54:9, the Lord says, "*For as the heavens are higher than the earth, so are my ways higher than your ways, and my thoughts than your thoughts.*" God has called you and I to a *high* calling, a *higher* way of thinking, a *higher* way of living, a life filled with meaning, significance, and purpose. That is the same kind of life to which God called Abram. Say these words out loud again: *"My season has changed."*

It is important to note that Abram lived before Calvary, so God was inviting him to find his higher life by being in a sacred partnership with Almighty God. That partnership eventually resulted in the birth, life, death, resurrection, and ascension of Jesus, the Messiah, the Seed of the Woman, the Seed of Abraham. God used Abram's faith and faithful obedience to bring to pass the very fulfillment of the Lamb slain from the foundation of the world (see Revelation 13:8).

But we, too, are invited into sacred partnership with the Almighty God. Even though the part of the plan that resulted *in* the Cross has already been accomplished, there is still a part of the plan that is a result *of* the Cross, and it is being worked out in the earth even today. On *this* side of the Cross, God is offering you and me the same kind of opportunity He did to Abram—the privilege of being involved in His redemptive plans and purposes. What an amazing opportunity!

We are invited to turn from our version of Babylon and follow Jesus. We are commanded and commissioned to be salt and light, to preach the Gospel to the ends of the earth, to lay hands on the sick, to cast out demons, to reach a lost and dying world for Jesus's sake. Yes, God offers us, too, an alternative to the ordinary low life and extends to us an extraordinary high life, filled with divine purpose and meaning.

Right now, He is revealing to you a fresh route to a new and dynamic future. Like Abram, you are not bound by nature or nurture, your genetics, or your upbringing. Like Abram, you were made for more.

A Parallel

There is a parallel to the Abraham narrative tucked away in Matthew 16:13–19. Notice

> When Jesus came into the region of Caesarea Philippi, He asked His disciples, saying, "Who do men say that I, the Son of Man, am?" So they said, "Some say John the Baptist, some Elijah, and others Jeremiah or one of the prophets." He said to them, "But who do you say that I am?" Simon Peter answered and said, "You are the Christ, the Son of the

living God." Jesus answered and said to him, "Blessed are you, Simon Bar Jonah, for flesh and blood has not revealed this to you, but My Father who is in heaven. And I also say to you that you are Peter, and on this rock I will build My church, and the gates of Hades shall not prevail against it. And I will give you the keys of the kingdom of heaven, and whatever you bind on earth will be bound in heaven, and whatever you loose on earth will be loosed in heaven."

When Simon blurted out the profound truth that the "Son of Man" is the "Son of God," Jesus was quick to point out this was an insight He did not get from his earthly father, whose name was John (not to be confused with John the Disciple or John the Baptist). That is why Jesus said, "*Blessed are you, Simon Bar Jonah.*" He was saying, "*Blessed are you, Simon, son of John.*" He went on to say, "Flesh and blood has not revealed this to you but My Father Who is in heaven." The idea is this, Simon's heavenly Father was offering him an alternative to the low life, and it was, of course, the high life. Simon's earthly father taught him how to fish, run a business, pay the bills and work hard, but all of that was outside of the purview of God's redemptive plans and purposes. Simon's heavenly Father afforded him a life that centered around the Son of Man, who was, of course, the Son of God. The parallel between Simon and Abram is remarkable. We will see more of their similarities in chapter 5.

A Tale of Two Cities

There are two extremely significant cities in the Bible. They are alluded to and mentioned directly all throughout scripture, and they are loaded with symbolism, metaphor, and allegory. The two cities are Babylon and the New Jerusalem. Babylon is man-made. It is the best man can do. It represents the arrogance of man, his fallen nature and weaknesses, which are profoundly exploited by hell. The New Jerusalem is God-made. It is the best God can do. It represents all that is right and good about God, and the fact that Jesus is the King of Kings, the King of Shalom, the Prince of Peace.

God appeared to Abram and said essentially, "I'm going to show you a city that is not man-made like Babylon. Rather, I'm going to show you a city that is God-made. I have laid its foundation and it is far superior to anything Nimrod or Terah could ever create." (See Hebrews 11:10.) In Revelation 18:10, we get the ultimate view of Babylon, and it is one of judgment and finality, "Alas, alas, that great city Babylon, that mighty city! For in one hour your judgment has come." But the New Jerusalem is the eternal, forever blessed headquarters of the King of Kings. "Of the increase of His government and peace there shall be no end" (Isa. 9:7).

In ancient Babylon, the devil successfully highjacked the concept of the one true and living God and His redemptive plan. Satan took full advantage of man's rebellion and hard-heartedness, resulting in God's being painted out of the picture. Man lost God, and by losing God, he lost himself. The identity of God was obscured and so was the identity of man. This fact guaranteed Abram's generation a brutal existence on the face of the earth.

Solomon described this situation in Ecclesiastes 4:1–3.

> Then I returned and considered all the oppression that is done under the sun: And look! The tears of the oppressed, but they have no comforter—on the side of their oppressors there is power, but they have no comforter. Therefore I praised the dead who were already dead, more than the living who are still alive. Yet, better than both is he who has never existed, who has not seen the evil work that is done under the sun.

The writer says it would have been better to have never existed than to live in such oppressive conditions. Man was doomed to live outside the purview of God's redemptive plans and purposes, with absolutely no power to resist the influences of the evil one. C. S. Lewis put it like this, "It [was] always winter but never Christmas." (Of course, this makes more sense in the northern hemisphere.) The idea is this: nobody was living for God. There was no man or woman living a life animated by God's redemptive purpose. Practically, every human being was living the low life, as a pawn in the hands of God's archenemy, the devil. It was hell on earth.

And then, one day, on the plains of Shinar, at the very gates of hell, to a man who seemed to be entrapped by a godless culture, God began to speak. Look at Genesis 12:1–6.

> Now the Lord had said to Abraham: "Get out of your country, from your family and from your father's house, to

a land that I will show you. I will make you a great nation; I will bless you and make your name great; and you shall be a blessing. I will bless those who bless you, and I will curse him who curses you; and in you all the families of the earth shall be blessed." So Abram departed as the Lord had spoken to him, and Lot went with him. And Abraham *was* seventy-five years old when he departed from Haran. Then Abraham took Sarai his wife and Lot his brother's son, and all their possessions that they had gathered, and the people whom they had acquired in Haran, and they departed to go to the land of Canaan. So they came to the land of Canaan. Abraham passed through the land to the place of Shechem, as far as the terebinth tree of Moreh. And the Canaanites *were* then in the land.

Essentially, God was saying, "Look around you, Abram, none of this will be yours! I'm giving you something entirely different, something you can't get from your earthly father!" Hebrews 11:8 puts it this way, "By faith Abram obeyed when he was called to go out to the place which he would receive as an inheritance." This inheritance would not come from Terah but from the Almighty God. God was saying, "I have to get you out of Babylon, but don't worry, Abram, although you will lose your Babylonian inheritance, I've got another inheritance for you. And it will not only change everything about you, it will change the world!" He was saying, "Abram, your *past* offers you Babylon, but I'm offering you a city whose builder and maker is God." (See Hebrews 11:10). What Abram's earthly father offered him was nothing compared to what Abram's heavenly Father offered him!

Abram was seventy-five years old when he was called to leave all he had ever known and follow a God he had only just met. And remarkably, he did it, and he continued following God until he died, one hundred years later. It was a monumental achievement! God came to Abram, right where he was, in an idol-making family and idol-worshiping culture, and summoned him out of the ordinary into the extraordinary.

God called him to greatness and blessing. Notice verses 2 and 3: "'I will make you a GREAT nation; I will BLESS you and make your name GREAT; and you shall be a BLESSING. I will BLESS those who bless you, and I will curse him who curses you; and in you all the families of the earth shall be BLESSED.'" This was a heavenly calling, a high calling to a high life. Abram had no idea *how* this would be worked out. All he knew was that God had made him promises that were just too good not pursue. He had to go for it. This was his moment.

However, this walking with God business was all brand new to him, and as we will see, he made a lot of mistakes along the way. And the Bible is careful to record them all. Aren't you glad your story is not in the Bible? Abram messed up from the get-go. When God asked him to leave all that was familiar to him, including the land and his father's household, he left the land, yes, but he invited his father, Terah, his brother Haran, and his nephew Lot. He dragged along pretty much the entirety of what was left of his father's household. In other words, he left his *land* but not his *clan*.

But knowing the background of his family, it becomes quite apparent that when God said, "Leave your family behind," He was saying, "I'm trying to separate you from their *mind-set*. Abram, their thinking has crippled them and held them back for ten generations. I'm trying to expose you to a larger world, to a bigger worldview, to a higher way of thinking, to My plans and purposes, to My redemptive calling." But by dragging his family along, Abram was inviting their mind-set along, too. Their old way of thinking was a hindrance to Abram and delayed his ability to fully grasp what God was trying to reveal to him and wanting to accomplish through him.

Abram would finally get his perspective right. Eventually, he took the limits off God and what God could do through him and Sarai. But years later, his descendants struggled with those same early struggles of their patriarch, Abram. Verse 41 of Psalm 78 says the children of Israel "limited the Holy One of Israel." God had called them into the Promised Land to dominate and thrive as a people. Yet when they peeked in, they were seized by fear because they saw their own abilities as superior to God's Word. They limited God's ability to enhance their abilities, to put his "super" on their "natural," and give them dominion over all the enemies that occupied the space God had promised to them.

From Abram's failures, and his descendants, too, the lesson for us is quite clear. We must guard against the tyranny of a colloquial mind-set—one that is based solely on the wisdom of man, what the mind and senses can deduce, figure, and determine. When our thinking is based on the aggregated and generally accepted wisdom of the day instead of what God has said, those worldly thoughts become a ruthless and relentless dictator. And like Nimrod, they will beat us down into believing God is unreliable and what He has promised is impossible. That mind-set will cut us off from His promises. And in turn, it will cause us to influence others to live the same way. If unchecked, it will become a generational curse, a stronghold that will prevent us and our children from stepping out beyond our comfort zone and into the very promises of God.

Interestingly, God spoke things to Abram at the very beginning that became the core of his pursuit. Primarily, the driving force in his pursuit of the promises was to have a son with Sarai. And although he had missteps all along the way, and it took twenty-five years to get there. He never relented.

Abram left his land, and eventually his clan, he quit worshiping other gods, defeated kings, and kingdoms; communed with God; covenanted with God; entertained angels and the Lord Himself; and he was incredibly blessed and prosperous. But it was the core promise of having a son with Sarai that drove him.

When you first become a Christian, I am convinced God speaks things to you. He puts dreams, visions, and desires deep inside you. He encodes them into your spiritual DNA, and even deeper. They are who you are at an atomic level. They are what drives you. They are your true self, who you really are. They are your calling and connect you to His plans and purposes. They are redemptive in nature and will help push His agenda forward in the earth. Do not underestimate them. Even though they may not have come to pass yet, that does not mean they will not. Your day will come. It is a process.

But here is an astounding truth—the twenty-four-year pursuit of a promise yielded blessings all along the way. *Even though the one promise he was after most did not manifest for over twenty years, from the moment he began pursuing it, he was blessed.* His life was lifted by the pursuit, in spite of the fact that the initial, primary promise was unfulfilled for the first twenty-five percent of the journey.

Then God put His promises in a language Abram could understand—the language of the blood covenant.

Catching a Glimpse

Turn your eyes upon Jesus
Look full in His wonderful face
And the things of earth will grow strangely dim
In the light of His glory and grace
—Helen Hawarth Lamel

Some friends of mine have served the Lord for many years in the wonderful country of Lithuania. When their oldest son was just a toddler, he pulled in really close to his father's face, looked intently into his eyes, and said, "Daddy, I can see me in your eyes." When we get really close to our heavenly Father and look intently into His eyes, not only do we see Him, we see *us*. We begin to catch the vision of His redemptive plans and where we fit into them. We become aware who He has called us to be. We see our true self in His eyes.

Something powerful happens when we look *away* from whatever we have looked to and we look to the Lord. David said, "*I will lift up my eyes to the hills. From whence cometh my help? My help comes from the Lord who made heaven and earth*" (Ps. 121:1–2). The significance of looking away *from* something and looking *towards* something else cannot be overstated. Ask Lot's wife. She refused to look away from Sodom and towards God's redemptive plan (Gen. 19:26). Even Jesus said, "Remember Lot's wife" (Luke 17:32). You will move in whatever direction you are looking. Try driving your car in one direction while looking in another. You will definitely drift in the direction you are looking (upon second thought, do not try this).

James 4:8 says, "Draw near to God and He will draw near to you." At first glance, this verse seems to indicate that *we* initiate the movement, but throughout the Bible, we see that it is God who moves first. Grace always precedes faith. He gets our attention in whatever way He must and, at that point, we have a choice to make. Will we turn and move toward Him or continue moving in the direction we were already headed? Will we choose to go our own way or let Him direct our paths? Jesus said in Matthew 5:8, *"Blessed are the pure in heart for they shall see God."* We are called to turn from the distractions of this world to Jesus and with a singularity of heart draw near to and focus on Him. As we are faithful to do this, we see Him in an intimate and purposeful way. Proximity *to* Him determines our perception *of* Him. And in seeing Him, we see our true self.

That is what happened with Moses and the burning bush some six hundred years after Abram. God initiated the whole encounter by setting the bush ablaze. It was close enough for him to see it but far away enough that Moses had to turn and intentionally pursue it. When he saw the bush burning and not being consumed, he had to decide: would he move closer to the fire or not? In Exodus 3:3, he said, "I will now turn aside and see this great sight." God initiated the movement by getting Moses's attention. Then Moses moved in for a closer look; as he drew near, he got a glimpse of God. God gave him insight into His plans, and by drawing closer to God, Moses also saw his place in God's plans, like the boy saw himself when he looked into his father's eyes.

Now, let us go back to Abram. God appeared to him in Babylonian Ur, gave him instructions, and invited him to be part of His cosmic plan to rescue humanity (see Genesis 12:1–3). Upon this encounter, Abram began to move towards God. It is important to note that the phrase "[he] believed God and it was counted to him as righteousness" describes another encounter that happens three chapters later, in Genesis 15. But if you take into consideration other scriptures such as Romans 4:3, Galatians 3:6, James 2:23, you can see that from the time God started talking to Abram, he believed and obeyed—at least to some extent, to the best of his ability. And as Abram moved towards God, God moved towards him. That becomes abundantly apparent in what God does next.

The Blood Covenant

To help solidify Abram's faith, He took the extraordinary step of encapsulating His redemptive vision into a format familiar to Abram. God put His promise into a legal instrument that was an acceptable means of conducting business during the time of Abram. That is, God put his redemptive promise into the form of a blood covenant.

He had spoken—that should have been enough. But God *propped up* His Word, at least in the eyes of Abram, by swearing an oath and shedding blood. In the customs of that day, this was the most powerful way God could assure Abram that what He had promised, He could and would perform. The dream of a son born to him and Sarai now came with a guarantee, so to speak—the blood covenant. But to really grasp the gravity of this transaction and why it meant so much to Abram, we need to take a deeper look at the idea of blood covenant.

Covenant was God's idea. Vestiges of it can be seen all the way back to the dawn of humanity, when God confronted Adam and Eve in the Garden of Eden after the fall. They had fashioned fancy little fig leaves for themselves, and God made it abundantly clear that fig leaves were not enough.

He called them into account, got them to admit their misdeeds, and then proceeded to curse the ground, the woman, the man, and the serpent. In Genesis 3:15, God dropped a thermonuclear bomb on hell. He promised the victorious Messiah. *"The Seed of the Woman will crush the head of the serpent."* Theologians call this the *protoevangelium*, or the first mention of the Gospel in the Scriptures. He was telling this prototypical couple—*"the woman will have a Son, and that Son will reverse the Curse."*

Now, they did not fully grasp this. As a matter of fact, they thought Cain was *that* son. And when they had Abel, they thought it could have been either one. They were certainly mistaken. I might add that the devil thought the same thing. And when he inspired Cain to kill Abel, he killed two birds with one stone, knocking them both out of contention.

But neither Cain nor Abel was the one. And neither was Seth. That promised son would not appear for another four thousand years, and his name would be Jesus. The idea, however, is this: when God was dealing with Adam and Eve in the garden, He let them know, redemption requires more than fig leaves. It required blood. So the great Creator of life did the unthinkable. He slaughtered and skinned animals and covered Adam and Eve in those skins.

Can you imagine the shock and horror as the first couple watched their heavenly father destroy these innocent animals? Adam and Eve had never witnessed death, much less, the violence and brutality required to obtain these skins.

When I was a kid, I would go hunting with my father, my grandfather, and my uncles. I remember the way I felt when I first saw dead squirrels and deer. I kind of studied them. They had been jumping around, going about their lives, when all of a sudden—boom!—and it was over. The finality of it all was sobering (I was a weird kid). But that was nothing compared to the gruesome process of gutting and skinning the critters. This must have been a nightmare to Adam and Eve. They exited paradise by way of a slaughterhouse. I believe those hides were un-tanned, in order to drive home the epic-ness of the fall, and the severity required to undo it. Adam and Eve caught a visceral glimpse of redemption's price.

And then, God taught them how to approach Him. They would do so with altars and sacrifices. In the same fashion as God in the garden, they would kill animals and then call on the name of the Lord, trusting Him for their ultimate redemption. The scripture makes it clear that they turned around and taught their boys to do the same. The point is this: by building altars, offering sacrifices, and calling on the name of the Lord, Adam and Eve and their children were expressing a deep and abiding faith in what God had promised—"The Seed of the woman will crush the head of the serpent." They were looking forward to the Cross, where the Seed of the woman would indeed crush the head of the serpent. And in a sense, we do the same thing on this side of the Cross. They put their faith in what He was going to do. We put our faith in what He has already done. Albeit, we do not kill animals because He is the Lamb that was slain, but our faith is the same.

But notice the next generation. Look at Genesis 4:3–5.

> And in the process of time it came to pass that Cain brought an offering of the fruit of the ground to the LORD. Abel also brought of $_c$ the firstborn of his flock and of their fat. And the LORD respected Abel and his offering, but He did not respect Cain and his offering. And Cain was very angry, and his countenance fell.

They were following the pattern their parents had taught them. They would in turn pass it on from generation to generation. In the process of time, the pattern would become part and parcel of the way people not only dealt with God, but each other. It is reasonable to assume that the ritual of killing animals and swearing oaths became a cultural norm to primal humanity. Varying forms of this process were used to conduct business, establish alliances, allegiances, and treaties. The blood covenant was how humanity strengthened bonds amongst themselves and formed abiding interpersonal relationships. Anthropologists have discovered the cutting of blood covenants and the swearing of oaths in virtually every people group on the face of the earth.

Interestingly, since Seth, one of Adam's sons, was alive when Noah was alive, we can deduce that whatever Adam knew, Abram could have known with only three intermediaries. (For more on this, see Phillip Rosenbaum's book, *How to Enjoy the Boring Parts of the Bible*.) It is quite apparent that the idea of blood covenant was a well-known, established concept during the time of Abram. In his exposition of Genesis 15, Matthew Henry is careful to point out that

Abram was "so well versed in the law and customs of sacrifices that he needed not any particular instructions…[for] he well knew the manner in preparing them" (Matthew Henry, *Commentary on the Whole Bible*).

Not only had God revealed Himself to Abram and declared who He had called Abram to be, but God also strengthened Abram's understanding and faith by putting His promises in the form of a blood covenant. This happened just a few years into Abraham's walk with God. Let us unpack the verses where God took this extraordinary step to help Abram become the man God said he could be.

Blurry Vision

Let's take a look at the events surrounding this encounter. Notice Genesis 15:1.

> After these things the word of the LORD came to Abram in a vision, saying, "Do not be afraid, Abram. I am your shield, your exceedingly great reward."

In Genesis 14, Abram had defeated a confederacy of four kings with just 318 men and was expecting retaliation from these kings. He had also refused payment for services rendered from the king of Sodom (See Genesis 14:21–24). So God was saying to him in that moment, "There's no need to be afraid, Abram. I am your protection and reward!" I love the fact He added "exceeding great" to the reward part, meaning, "whatever the king of Sodom offered you is nothing compared to Me!" It's like He was saying, "Do you want the golden egg or the goose that lays the golden egg?" Not that I am comparing God to a goose! You get the point.

Notice verse 2,

> But Abram said, "Lord GOD, what will You give me, seeing I go childless, and the heir of my house is Eliezer of Damascus?"

Abram caught a glimpse of the Lord back in Ur, His redemptive vision and his own place in it, and because he had pursued that vision, God had richly blessed him. At this point in his journey, ten years or so into it, he was wealthy beyond his wildest dreams, powerful, wise, and influential. But the natural reality of his being "childless" was greater to him than the Word of God that said, "You are a father of many nations." He was struggling to clearly see himself the way God already saw him. Abram's vision was impaired, limited. Abram's vision was blurry.

Verses 3 to 8 show us what God did next.

> Then Abram said, "Look, You have given me no offspring; indeed one born in my house is my heir!" And behold, the word of the LORD came to him, saying, "This one shall not be your heir, but one who will come from your own body shall be your heir." Then He brought him outside and said, "Look now toward heaven, and count the stars if you are able to number them." And He said to him, "So shall your descendants be." And he believed in the LORD, and He accounted it to

> him for righteousness. Then He said to him, "I am the LORD, who brought you out of Ur of the Chaldeans, to give you this land to inherit it." And he said, "Lord GOD, how shall I know that I will inherit it?"

God gave Abram a visual. He was trying to get Abram to clearly see himself as a father with generations of offspring. So God showed him the stars. Abram could see only about three thousand stars on a clear night. God let him know He was bringing him into a land, a place that his descendants would inherit. But still, after the stars and the promise of a homeland, Abram essentially said, in verse 8, "I need an assurance!"

So God gave him the assurance he needed by putting His promise in a language he well understood—blood covenant. Notice verses 9 to 19.

> So He said to him, "Bring Me a three-year-old heifer, a three-year-old female goat, a three-year-old ram, a turtledove, and a young pigeon." Then he brought all these to Him and cut them in two, down the middle, and placed each piece opposite the other; but he did not cut the birds in two. And when the vultures came down on the carcasses, Abram drove them away. Now when the sun was going down, a deep sleep fell upon Abram; and behold, horror and great darkness fell upon him. Then He said to Abram: "Know certainly that your

descendants will be strangers in a land that is not theirs, and will serve them, and they will afflict them four hundred years. "And also the nation whom they serve I will judge; afterward they shall come out with great possessions. Now as for you, you shall go to your fathers in peace; you shall be buried at a good old age. But in the fourth generation they shall return here, for the iniquity of the Amorites is not yet complete." And it came to pass, when the sun went down and it was dark, that behold, there appeared a smoking oven and a burning torch that passed between those pieces. On the same day the LORD made a covenant with Abram, saying: "To your descendants I have given this land, from the river of Egypt to the great river, the River Euphrates—"the Kenites, the Kenezzites, the Kadmonites, the Hittites, the Perizzites, the Rephaim, the Amorites, the Canaanites, the Girgashites, and the Jebusites."

Interestingly, over time, the death of the animals had come to mean something different than what was originally intended in the Edenic sacrifices. Here we see the death of the animals, meaning, "If I fail to perform what I have sworn in this covenant agreement, then let it be unto me as has been done unto these animals." Another way of seeing the sacrifice was this: "As this animal has died, so I have died to self, and now I live in union with my covenant partner." These are poignant and powerful images, rich in symbolism. (For more information on covenant, I recommend the nineteenth century classic by H. Clay Trumball, entitled *The Blood Covenant*.) When God swore an oath and sealed it in the blood of animals, Abram understood Him to say: "*I will do what I have declared! I really Am who I say I Am and you really are who I say you are!*" Abram got the assurance he needed.

This goes beyond a mere contract. Catholic theologian, Scott Hahn, highlights the difference between a contract and a covenant. In his book, *A Father Who Keeps His Promises*, Hahn correctly notes that in a contract, you make an agreement and sign on the dotted line, but in a covenant, you make promises and swear oaths.

Dr. Hahn points out that modern contracts are so far beneath ancient covenants that "contracts are like prostitution and covenants are like marriage. Contracts are like slavery, covenants are like sonship" (Scott Hahn, Salvation History: One Holy Family, at www.star.ucl.ac.uk/~vgg/rc/aplgtc/hahn/m2/slvhst1.html).

Hebrews 6:13–18 says,

> For when God made a promise to Abraham, because He could swear by no one greater, He swore by Himself, saying, "Surely blessing I will bless you, and multiplying I will multiply you." And so, after he had patiently endured, he obtained the promise. For men indeed swear by the greater, and an oath for confirmation *is* for them an end of all dispute. Thus God, determining to show more abundantly to the heirs of promise the immutability of His counsel, confirmed *it* by an oath, that by two immutable things,

> in which it *is* impossible for God to lie, we might have strong consolation, who have fled for refuge to lay hold of the hope set before *us*.

In times past, in an American court of law, one would place their hand on a Bible and swear an oath. The ritual went something like this, "Do you swear to tell the truth and nothing but the truth, so help you God?" The response was, "I swear." The idea was this: "I am swearing by a higher power to tell the truth, and if I fail to tell the truth, then I will answer to this higher power."

When God swore an oath, there was no higher power by whom He could swear. So He swore by Himself. The initial promise God made to Abram was unchanging (immutable), and the oath He swore was, too. God's promise and oath are the two things the writer refers to in Hebrews 6:18. Nevertheless, *for Abram's sake*, God moved beyond the promise to the oath.

One might think that after Abram was brought into this sacred covenant relationship with the Almighty God, he would have gotten his act together, and he and Sarai would have had that son. But that is not what happened at all—which should give all of us hope! Abram was a human being just like the rest of us. He put his pants on one leg at a time (as my grandmother used to say). He was garden-variety, salt-of-the-earth, normal, average flesh and blood. We know this because immediately on the heels of this covenant, Sarai moved beyond the age of childbearing and suggested to Abram that he have a son with her Egyptian handmaiden, Hagar. And that is exactly what he did.

When I was a kid, my father would take me fishing. He was from the country and loved to fish the old-fashioned way, with cane poles. Sometimes in the Louisiana sun, when the fish were not biting, I would take the end of my cane pole and begin to push my cork down under the water to make it look like I was getting a bite. I was cheating. It does not work that way. When it came to the Hagar debacle, Abram was cheating. That was not the plan. Abram was trying to "make" the miracle happen, rather than trusting God.

Fourteen years later, it became quite obvious this second-wife thing had been one big mistake. To keep peace in the home, and to protect the promise, Abram ended up having to send Hagar and Ishmael away. Again, notice, Abram wasted even more time. He had failed once again. But Abram was never defined by his failure.

Finally, as the years slipped by, both Sarai and Abram lost their ability to have a child. And it was then, when it seemed all hope was gone, that God met with Abram again. This time, however, everything shifted. He had just begun to catch a glimpse of who God had called him to be. That is when God catalyzed the process and gave him a means, whereby, he began to see more clearly and completely just who he really was, and the results rocked the world.

The Catalyst

I am chosen not forsaken
I am who You say I am
You are for me not against me
I am who You say I am

—Hillsong Worship,
"I Am Who You Say I Am"

There is a tipping point in the story of Abram. Within ninety days of this tipping point, Sarai was pregnant. Within a year she and Abram were holding their promised son. They had waited on him since they had left Babylonian Ur some twenty-four years earlier. And during those waiting years, their bodies gradually aged out, and the unlikely possibility of them having a son became an absolute impossibly, that is until this tipping point. Something happened that activated the promise, altered them physiologically, and the miracle that had been so elusive suddenly manifested. What was that "something," that catalyst? Is it possible for you and me to experience this same kind of catalyst? Is it possible for yet-to-be-fulfilled promises in our lives to suddenly be activated and quickly manifest?

The catalyst Abram and Sarai experienced was powerful enough to bring about almost *immediate* results. Again, after twenty-four years of waiting, within ninety days, she was pregnant. I am convinced there are promises God has made you that have been lying dormant, maybe for years. They are like sticks of dynamite waiting for a spark. How would you like to have an explosive manifestation of God's promises in your life? At the risk of sounding hyperbolic, what you will discover in this chapter has the power to do just that. Let's begin in Romans 4:16–7.

> Therefore it is of faith that it might be according to grace, so that the promise might be sure to all the seed, not only to those who are of the law, but also to those who are of the faith of Abraham, who is the father of us all (as it is written, "I have made you a father of many nations") in the presence of Him whom he believed—God, who gives life to the dead and calls those things which do not exist as though they did.

Ultimately, verses 16 and 17 are saying that it is by faith that we receive anything from God, whether we are ethnic descendants of Abram (Jews) or not (Gentiles). *Abram* and *Abraham* are names for the same guy. We will cover that soon enough. But notice verse 17. It concludes by saying God *"gives life to the dead and calls those things which do not exist as though they did."*

By the time Isaac was conceived, Abram was already *"dead."* In other words, he could not produce a son. And for that matter, neither could Sarah. But verse 17 gives us a hint as to *how* God brought life out of death. First, pay attention to the first two phrases—(1) God *"calls things."* And (2) God calls *"things which do not exist."* Now notice, He calls things which do not exist *as if they actually do exist*. And how does He call them? With *words*. *He speaks things that do not exist into being.* Is not this the way God started it all? Genesis 1:1 tells us that when God looked at noncreation, He literally said, "Light be." He called a thing (light) that was not as though it actually was. How? With His words. This principle of using words to "call those things which do not exist as though they did" is the fundamental component of Abram's catalyst.

Take a closer look at what Romans 4:19–21 says regarding the miracle of Isaac's birth.

> And not being weak in faith, he did not consider his own body, already dead (since he was about a hundred years old), and the deadness of Sarah's womb. He did not waver at the promise of God through unbelief, but was strengthened in faith, giving glory to God, and being fully convinced that what He had promised He was also able to perform.

Notice the five things these verses reveal about our man, Abram.

1. He was not "*weak in faith*" (verse 19).
2. Verse 19 says, "He did not consider his own body, already dead…and the deadness of Sarah's womb." That sounds like he ignored reality, but the Greek conveys quite the opposite idea. The New International Version more accurately reflects the original language. It says "…*he faced the fact that his body was as good as dead…and that Sarah's womb*

was also dead." And in spite of his looking grim reality in the face, he was "*not weak in faith*" and "*did not waver at the promise of God through unbelief*" (verse 20).
3. He "*was strengthened in faith*" (verse 20).
4. He "[gave] *glory to God*" for something that had not yet manifested (verse 20).
5. He was "*fully convinced that what God had promised He was able to perform*" (verse 21).

That sounds *nothing* like the guy in Genesis 15 and 16. Back in Genesis 15, God cut a covenant with Abram and swore that he and Sarai would have a son. We saw how powerful this was in the previous chapter. But right on the heels of that, in Genesis 16, Abram married Hagar and had Ishmael. I would say this is a prime example of what it means to be "*weak in faith*"! I mean, Abram compromised the precision of God's promise, that said he and *Sarai* would have a son—*not* he and Hagar. The debacle of Genesis 16 certainly qualifies Abram as being one who "*waver*[ed] *at the promises of God through unbelief*" and paints a picture of someone who was *not* "*strengthened in faith.*" And in Genesis 16, Abram was definitely *not* "*giving glory to God*" for a yet-to-be-manifested promise. Finally, Genesis 16 categorically proves Abram was *not* "*fully convinced that what God had promised He was able to perform.*"

So why does Romans 4 seem to be describing a totally different man? Because it is describing Abram post-catalyst! The parenthetical expression in Romans 4:19 is the key to discovering what brought him from weak faith that *could not* produce Isaac to an unstoppable faith that *could* produce Isaac, even in the face of absolute impossibility! Romans 4:18–21 says Abram was *not* weak in faith, *unwavering* in the face of overwhelming obstacles, *grew stronger and stronger* in faith and praised God for Isaac *in advance*, because he was *fully convinced* that what God had promised was inevitable "*when he was about a hundred years old.*"

God called him at seventy-five years of age. These statements from Romans 4 do not describe the seventy-five-year-old, eighty-three-year-old, ninety-five-year-old, or ninety-eight-year-old Abram. The Bible says *when he was about one hundred*. At ninety-nine, there was a catalyst that caused his faith to soar, and the world would never be the same.

Cause and Effect: The Means to an End

So what happened? What brought about the catalyst? *God changed his name*. Do not gloss over this. This is *the* integral ingredient that changed everything. We dare not relegate this to fanciful idioms and allegories. The name change was very real, practical and down-to-earth. It had to be fleshed out in everyday life. It was an ingenious mechanism designed and engineered by the promise-giver Himself for the specific purpose of causing a spark to bring about explosive faith in the promise-receiver. It was classic *cause and effect*, the *means to an end*. This simple linguistic device catapulted Abram and Sarai into being possessors of their promises. It was the epicenter of a spiritual earthquake, the aftershocks of which we feel to this day. Let us dive in a little deeper.

Look at Genesis 17:1–6:

> When Abram was ninety-nine years old, the LORD appeared to Abraham and said to him, "I am Almighty God; walk before Me and be blameless. And

I will make My covenant between Me and you, and will multiply you exceedingly." Then Abram fell on his face, and God talked with him, saying: "As for Me, behold, My covenant is with you, and you shall be a father of many nations. No longer shall your name be called Abram, but your name shall be Abraham; for I have made you a father of many nations. I will make you exceedingly fruitful; and I will make nations of you, and kings shall come from you."

In verse 15, God changed Sarai's name to "Sarah." Technically, Abram and Sarai both got a piece of the name "*Jehovah.*" This was part of the ritual of covenant cutting. We see remnants of this even today. For instance, when a couple enters the covenant of marriage, customarily the bride takes the name of the groom. This is an echo of an ancient day. Incidentally, in a sense, God got a piece of Abraham's name, too, in that He became known as "the God of Abraham."

The name *Abram* means, "father of height or stature," while the name *Abraham* means, "father of multitudes." God wanted Abram to call himself exactly and precisely what God had always called him: the father of multitudes. It was almost a legalistic technicality. The names were similar but not identical. God was splitting hairs, crossing the *T*s and dotting the *I*s. But for Abram to have the ability to produce the promise, he had to carefully construe his language in such a way that matched his destiny. He had to consistently speak words that were congruent to his calling. Abram had to linguistically self-identify in such a way as to reflect and project faith in the Word of God that had been spoken over him.

Think about that. For nearly one hundred years, he had self-identified as "Abram." Others knew him as "Abram." His camels, cattle, and credit cards were in that name. His bank accounts and business dealings were in that name. His titles, deeds, and contracts were in that name. Then suddenly it all had to change. Think of the hassle. I remember the trouble my wife, Valerie, went to when she legally changed her last name to "Hill." And she was only twenty. Imagine ninety-nine years' worth of business dealings. But if Abraham was to ever see the manifestation of God's promise, this kind of careful attention to detail was an absolute necessity.

Abram had to intentionally, and inconveniently, correct people when they called him by his ninety-nine-year-old name. "Literally, when someone said, "Hey, Abram!" he had to say, "That is not who I am. I am who I Am says I am-and I am Abraham-the father of multitudes." Think of the time that seemed wasted as this old man went to the trouble of changing his name. But then, consider the results. There was something so very powerful in that confession—power that unlocked the very promises of God—power that literally changed he and Sarah's physiological makeup.

Do you know what the word *confession* means? It comes from the Greek word *homologeo* and means "to say the same thing." What was Abraham doing every time he *called* himself Abraham? He was saying the same thing God had been saying about him from the beginning; hence, like God, *he was calling those things which do not exist as though they did.* Incidentally, the name *Sarai* means "princess to one" while *Sarah* means "princess to many." She had been Abram's princess and had limited authority with their entourage, but her sphere of influence and scope of authority had been made exponentially bigger. By changing her name, God compelled her to confess the truth of who she really was.

In chapter 3, we saw a parallel with Simon. Jesus told him, *"Blessed are you, Simon BarJonah, for flesh and blood has not revealed this to you, but My Father who is in heaven"* (Matthew 16:17). Jesus was letting him know that what Simon's own father had planned for him was being trumped by his heavenly Father. Jonah (John) had planned for Simon to be a successful fisherman, a businessman, an entrepreneur. But his heavenly Father had other plans. He was called to be an Apostle of the Lamb. He was destined to preach Pentecost in Acts 2. His mission was to open the door of the gospel to Jews and Gentiles alike. He was to write two books in the Bible. And guess what? God changed his name, too. In Matthew 16:18, Jesus said, *"And I also say to you that you are Peter, and on this rock I will build My church, and the gates of Hades shall not prevail against it."* The name *Simon* means "hear," but the name *Peter* means "rock." From the moment he received the profound revelation of Jesus's true identity, he began to see himself as God saw him. His earthly father had called him the "hearer," but his heavenly father had called him the "rock." Not only was he a flinty force in the propagation of the Gospel, he was and is a foundation stone for the church (see Ephesians 2:20). Revelation 21:14 even says one of the foundation stones of heaven bears the apostle's name. And since Jesus renamed him "Peter," we can be certain of which name is on that heavenly foundation stone. Like Abraham, his name was changed to correspond with his mission. The name and the mission were like hand-in-glove.

However, as we saw in chapter 1, when we begin to follow Jesus, we certainly do not have to change our name. But as Christians, we are considered to be "Abraham's seed and heirs according to the promise" (see Galatians 3:29). And like Abraham, there are things that we should be confessing regarding our true identity. Hebrews 10:23 says: "Let us hold fast the confession of our hope without wavering, for He who promised is faithful." Abraham, Sarah and Peter were *confessors* before they were *possessors*. It is absolutely vital that our words line up with His promises.

One Angel and Two People

Nothing makes this clearer than the story of one angel and two people. The angel, Gabriel, appeared to Zacharias while he was discharging his priestly duties in the temple complex. Notice Luke 1:8–23:

> So it was, that while he was serving as priest before God in the order of his division, according to the custom of the priesthood, his lot fell to burn incense when he went into the temple of the Lord. And the whole multitude of the people was praying outside at the hour of incense. Then an angel of the Lord appeared to him, standing on the right side of the altar of incense. And when Zacharias saw him, he was troubled, and fear fell upon him. But the angel said to him, "Do not be afraid, Zacharias, for your prayer is heard; and your wife Elizabeth will bear you a son, and you shall call his name John. And you will have joy and gladness, and many will rejoice at his birth. For he will be great in the sight of the Lord, and shall drink neither wine nor strong drink. He will also

be filled with the Holy Spirit, even from his mother's womb. And he will turn many of the children of Israel to the Lord their God. He will also go before Him in the spirit and power of Elijah, 'to turn the hearts of the fathers to the children,' and the disobedient to the wisdom of the just, to make ready a people prepared for the Lord." And Zacharias said to the angel, "How shall I know this? For I am an old man, and my wife is well advanced in years." And the angel answered and said to him, "I am Gabriel, who stands in the presence of God, and was sent to speak to you and bring you these glad tidings. But behold, you will be mute and not able to speak until the day these things take place, because you did not believe my words which will be fulfilled in their own time." And the people waited for Zacharias, and marveled that he lingered so long in the temple. But when he came out, he could not speak to them; and they perceived that he had seen a vision in the temple, for he beckoned to them and remained speechless. So it was, as soon as the days of his service were completed, that he departed to his own house.

Zacharias asked a question in unbelief. He was protesting and giving voice to his doubts. The "sign" that he was given was that he would not be able to give voice to his doubts anymore. He would be mute. This is fascinating.

His voice, which amplified his words and conveyed what was in his heart had the power to sabotage his promise. So the angel took that away from him. Jesus said, "Out of the abundance of the heart the mouth speaks" (Matt. 12:34). Proverbs 18:1a says, "Death and life are in the power of the tongue." Romans 10:17 tells us that "faith comes by hearing." Apparently doubt does too, or at least, faith can be hindered by words. It is better to say nothing at all than to give voice to your doubts. That is why in Joshua 6, the Lord commanded the children of Israel to march around the walls of Jericho, but Joshua told them not to say a word while they did so. He knew from personal experience that they would talk themselves out of their promise (see Numbers 13 and 14).

In Luke 1:26–38, the same angel appeared to Mary. Compare and contrast the two stories.

> Now in the sixth month the angel Gabriel was sent by God to a city of Galilee named Nazareth, to a virgin betrothed to a man whose name was Joseph, of the house of David. The virgin's name was Mary. And having come in, the angel said to her, "Rejoice, highly favored one, the Lord is with you; blessed are you among women!" But when she saw him, she was troubled at his saying, and considered what manner of greeting this was. Then the angel said to her, "Do not be afraid, Mary, for you have found favor with God. And behold, you will conceive in your womb and bring forth a Son, and shall call His name JESUS. He will be great, and will be called the Son of

the Highest; and the Lord God will give Him the throne of His father David. And He will reign over the house of Jacob forever, and of His kingdom there will be no end." Then Mary said to the angel, "How can this be, since I do not know a man?" And the angel answered and said to her, "The Holy Spirit will come upon you, and the power of the Highest will overshadow you; therefore, also, that Holy One who is to be born will be called the Son of God. Now indeed, Elizabeth your relative has also conceived a son in her old age; and this is now the sixth month for her who was called barren. For with God nothing will be impossible." Then Mary said, "Behold the maidservant of the Lord! Let it be to me according to your word." And the angel departed from her.

Mary asked a reasonable and logical question about how she, as a virgin, could have a child. And unlike her cousin's husband, Zacharias, she asked from a heart of faith, not doubt. The angel answered her question, and then she responded, revealing her heart of faith: "Behold the maidservant of the Lord! Let it be to me according to your word." Can you see the difference between Zacharias and Mary? His words were prohibitive while her words were permissive, actually helping to facilitate the promise.

I AM³

God Knew Abram Would Get It Eventually

Keep in mind, God did not write off Abram in the first or second decade of his faith walk because He knew eventually Abram would get it. I love that! God knew he would grow up, learn his lessons, and become the man God had called him to be. As a matter of fact, twenty-five years before Abraham got the name, Abraham, God had declared, "*I will make your name great*" (Gen. 12:2). Abraham did not even know the name "Abraham" when God said that. Maybe you have heard God whisper things into your spirit, but you have no idea just how much favor is packed into that still, small voice. You have yet to fully realize the greatness—the blessing—the favor of the Lord that He has spoken and declared over you. You have yet to realize how He sees you, and you are certainly not saying the same thing about yourself that He has said about you. Please hear this. God wants you to see yourself the way He sees you. And to make that happen, He will help you change the way you *talk* about yourself.

You may be thinking, "I don't know who He says I am, so how can I speak in agreement with Him?" My advice would be to start with the written Word, the Bible. To this world, you and I may not look like much, but as followers of Christ, our heavenly Father has made some staggering statements about us. There are over one hundred statements about who we are in Christ. These verses contain the phrasing, "in Christ," or some variant thereof, and express the truth about our identity. Here is a list of 163 such verses.

In Christ

Being justified freely by His grace through the redemption that is in Christ Jesus (Rom. 3:24)

Likewise you also, reckon yourselves to be dead indeed to sin, but alive to God in Christ Jesus our Lord. (Rom. 6:11)

There is therefore now no condemnation to those who are in Christ Jesus, who do not walk according to the flesh, but according to the Spirit. (Rom. 8:1)

For the law of the Spirit of life in Christ Jesus has made me free from the law of sin and death. (Rom. 8:2)

So we, being many, are one body in Christ, and individually members of one another. (Rom. 12:5)

To the church of God which is at Corinth, to those who are sanctified in Christ Jesus, called to be saints, with all who in every place call on the name of Jesus Christ our Lord, both theirs and ours. (1 Cor. 1:2)

I thank my God always concerning you for the grace of God which was given to you by Christ Jesus. (1 Cor. 1:4)

But of Him you are in Christ Jesus, who became for us wisdom from God—and righteousness and sanctification and redemption. (1 Cor. 1:30)

For as in Adam all die, even so in Christ all shall be made alive. (1 Cor. 15:22)

Now He who establishes us with you in Christ and has anointed us is God. (2 Cor. 1:21)

Now thanks be to God who always leads us in triumph in Christ, and through us diffuses the fragrance of His knowledge in every place. (2 Cor. 2:14)

But their minds were blinded. For until this day the same veil remains unlifted in the reading of the Old Testament, because the veil is taken away in Christ. (2 Cor. 3:14)

Therefore, if anyone is in Christ, he is a new creation; old things have passed away; behold, all things have become new. (2 Cor. 5:17)

That is, that God was in Christ reconciling the world to Himself, not imputing their trespasses to them, and has committed to us the word of reconciliation. (2 Cor. 5:19)

And this occurred because of false brethren secretly brought in (who came in by stealth to spy out our liberty which we have in Christ Jesus, that they might bring us into bondage. (Gal. 2:4)

Knowing that a man is not justified by the works of the law but by faith in Jesus Christ, even we have believed in Christ Jesus, that we might be justified by faith in Christ and not by the works of the law; for by the works of the law no flesh shall be justified. (Gal. 2:16)

For you are all sons of God through faith in Christ Jesus. (Gal. 3:26)

There is neither Jew nor Greek, there is neither slave nor free, there is neither male nor female; for you are all one in Christ Jesus. (Gal. 3:28)

For in Christ Jesus neither circumcision nor uncircumcision avails anything, but faith working through love. (Gal. 5:6)

For in Christ Jesus neither circumcision nor uncircumcision avails anything, but a new creation. (Gal. 6:15)

I AM[3]

Blessed be the God and Father of our Lord Jesus Christ, who has blessed us with every spiritual blessing in the heavenly places in Christ. (Eph. 1:3)

Just as He chose us in Him before the foundation of the world, that we should be holy and without blame before Him in love. (Eph. 1:4)

That in the dispensation of the fullness of the times He might gather together in one all things in Christ, both which are in heaven and which are on earth—in Him. (Eph. 1:10)

That we who first trusted in Christ should be to the praise of His glory. (Eph. 1:12)

And raised us up together, and made us sit together in the heavenly places in Christ Jesus. (Eph. 2:6

That in the ages to come He might show the exceeding riches of His grace in His kindness toward us in Christ Jesus. (Eph. 2:7)

For we are His workmanship, created in Christ Jesus for good works, which God prepared beforehand that we should walk in them. (Eph. 2:10)

But now in Christ Jesus you who once were far off have been brought near by the blood of Christ. (Eph. 2:13)

That the Gentiles should be fellow heirs, of the same body, and partakers of His promise in Christ through the gospel. (Eph. 3:6)

I press toward the goal for the prize of the upward call of God in Christ Jesus. (Phil. 3:14)

And the peace of God, which surpasses all understanding, will guard your hearts and minds through Christ Jesus. (Phil. 4:7)

I can do all things through Christ who strengthens me. (Phil. 4:13)

And my God shall supply all your need according to His riches in glory by Christ Jesus. (Phil. 4:19)

Him we preach, warning every man and teaching every man in all wisdom, that we may present every man perfect in Christ Jesus. (Col. 1:28)

For the Lord Himself will descend from heaven with a shout, with the voice of an archangel, and with the trumpet of God. And the dead in Christ will rise first. (1 Thess. 4:16)

In everything give thanks; for this is the will of God in Christ Jesus for you. (1 Thess. 5:18)

And the grace of our Lord was exceedingly abundant, with faith and love which are in Christ Jesus. (1 Tim. 1:14)

Paul, an apostle of Jesus Christ by the will of God, according to the promise of life which is in Christ Jesus. (2 Tim. 1:1)

Who has saved us and called us with a holy calling, not according to our works, but according to His own purpose and grace which was given to us in Christ Jesus before time began. (2 Tim. 1:9)

Hold fast the pattern of sound words which you have heard from me, in faith and love which are in Christ Jesus. (2 Tim. 1:13)

You therefore, my son, be strong in the grace that is in Christ Jesus. (2 Tim. 2:1)

Therefore I endure all things for the sake of the elect, that they also may obtain the salvation which is in Christ Jesus with eternal glory. (2 Tim. 2:10)

And that from childhood you have known the Holy Scriptures, which are able to make you wise for salvation through faith which is in Christ Jesus. (2 Tim. 3:15)

That the sharing of your faith may become effective by the acknowledgment of every good thing which is in you in Christ Jesus. (Philem. 1:6)

But may the God of all grace, who called us to His eternal glory by Christ Jesus, after you have suffered a while, perfect, establish, strengthen, and settle you. (1 Pet. 5:10)

In Him

In Him was life, and the life was the light of men. (John 1:4)

That whoever believes in Him should not perish but have eternal life. (John 3:15)

For God so loved the world that He gave His only begotten Son, that whoever believes in Him should not perish but have everlasting life. (John 3:16)

For in Him we live and move and have our being, as also some of your own poets have said, "For we are also His offspring." (Acts 17:28)

That you were enriched in everything by Him in all utterance and all knowledge. (1 Cor. 1:5)

For all the promises of God in Him are Yes, and in Him Amen, to the glory of God through us. (2 Cor. 1:20)

For He made Him who knew no sin to be sin for us, that we might become the righteousness of God in Him. (2 Cor. 5:21)

In Him we have redemption through His blood, the forgiveness of sins, according to the riches of His grace. (Eph. 1:7)

In Him also we have obtained an inheritance, being predestined according to the purpose of Him who works all things according to the counsel of His will. (Eph. 1:11)

n Him you also trusted, after you heard the word of truth, the gospel of your salvation; in whom also, having believed, you were sealed with the Holy Spirit of promise. (Eph. 1:13)

In whom the whole building, being fitted together, grows into a holy temple in the Lord. (Eph. 2:21)

In whom you also are being built together for a dwelling place of God in the Spirit. (Eph. 2:22)

And be found in Him, not having my own righteousness, which is from the law, but that which is through faith in Christ, the righteousness which is from God by faith. (Phil. 3:9)

For by Him all things were created that are in heaven and that are on earth, visible and invisible, whether thrones or dominions or principalities or powers. All things were created through Him and for Him. (Col. 1:16)

And He is before all things, and in Him all things consist. (Col. 1:17)

In whom are hidden all the treasures of wisdom and knowledge. (Col. 2:3)

Rooted and built up in Him and established in the faith, as you have been taught, abounding in it with thanksgiving. (Col. 2:7)

And you are complete in Him, who is the head of all principality and power. (Col. 2:10)

In Him you were also circumcised with the circumcision made without hands, by putting off the body of the sins of the flesh, by the circumcision of Christ. (Col. 2:11)

Having disarmed principalities and powers, He made a public spectacle of them, triumphing over them in it. (Col. 2:15)

But whoever keeps His word, truly the love of God is perfected in him. By this we know that we are in Him. (1 John 2:5)

He who says he abides in Him ought himself also to walk just as He walked. (1 John 2:6)

Again, a new commandment I write to you, which thing is true in Him and in you, because the darkness is passing away, and the true light is already shining. (1 John 2:8)

But the anointing which you have received from Him abides in you, and you do not need that anyone teach you; but as the same anointing teaches you concerning all things, and is true, and is not a lie, and just as it has taught you, you will abide in Him. (1 John 2:27)

And now, little children, abide in Him, that when He appears, we may have confidence and not be ashamed before Him at His coming. (1 John 2:28)

And everyone who has this hope in Him purifies himself, just as He is pure. (1 John 3:3)

Whoever abides in Him does not sin. Whoever sins has neither seen Him nor known Him. (1 John 3:6)

Now he who keeps His commandments abides in Him, and He in him. And by this we know that He abides in us, by the Spirit whom He has given us. (1 John 3:24)

By this we know that we abide in Him, and He in us, because He has given us of His Spirit. (1 John 4:13)

Now this is the confidence that we have in Him, that if we ask anything according to His will, He hears us. (1 John 5:14)

And if we know that He hears us, whatever we ask, we know that we have the petitions that we have asked of Him. (1 John 5:15)

And we know that the Son of God has come and has given us an understanding, that we may know Him who is true; and we are in Him who is true, in His Son Jesus Christ. This is the true God and eternal life. (1 John 5:20)

Whom having not seen you love. Though now you do not see Him, yet believing, you rejoice with joy inexpressible and full of glory. (1 Pet. 1:8)

In the Beloved

To the praise of the glory of His grace, by which He made us accepted in the Beloved. (Eph. 1:6)

In the Lord

For you were once darkness, but now you are light in the Lord. Walk as children of light. (Eph. 5:8)

Finally, my brethren, be strong in the Lord and in the power of His might. (Eph. 6:10)

In Whom

In whom we have boldness and access with confidence through faith in Him. (Eph. 3:12)

In whom we have redemption through His blood, the forgiveness of sins. (Col. 1:14)

By Christ

And you will be hated by all for My name's sake. But he who endures to the end shall be saved. (Mark 13:13)

You were bought at a price; do not become slaves of men. (1 Cor. 7:23)

For as by one man's disobedience many were made sinners, so also by one Man's obedience many will be made righteous. (Rom. 5:19)

And to make all see what is the fellowship of the mystery, which from the beginning of the ages has been hidden in

God who created all things through Jesus Christ. (Eph. 3:9)

Blessed be the God and Father of our Lord Jesus Christ, who according to His abundant mercy has begotten us again to a living hope through the resurrection of Jesus Christ from the dead. (1 Pet. 1:3)

Through Christ

Therefore, having been justified by faith, we have peace with God through our Lord Jesus Christ. (Rom. 5:1)

And not only that, but we also rejoice in God through our Lord Jesus Christ, through whom we have now received the reconciliation. (Rom. 5:11)

But the free gift is not like the offense. For if by the one man's offense many died, much more the grace of God and the gift by the grace of the one Man, Jesus Christ, abounded to many. (Rom. 5:15)

For if by the one man's offense death reigned through the one, much more those who receive abundance of grace and of the gift of righteousness will reign in life through the One, Jesus Christ. (Rom. 5:17)

For the wages of sin is death, but the gift of God is eternal life in Christ Jesus our Lord. (Rom. 6:23)

Therefore, my brethren, you also have become dead to the law through the body of Christ, that you may be married to another—to Him who was raised from the dead, that we should bear fruit to God. (Rom. 7:4)

But thanks be to God, who gives us the victory through our Lord Jesus Christ. (1 Cor. 15:57)

Now all things are of God, who has reconciled us to Himself through Jesus Christ, and has given us the ministry of reconciliation. (2 Cor. 5:18)

That the blessing of Abraham might come upon the Gentiles in Christ Jesus, that we might receive the promise of the Spirit through faith. (Gal. 3:14)

Therefore you are no longer a slave but a son, and if a son, then an heir of God through Christ. (Gal. 4:7)

Having predestined us to adoption as sons by Jesus Christ to Himself, according to the good pleasure of His will. (Eph. 1:5)

I AM[3]

Being filled with the fruits of righteousness which are by Jesus Christ, to the glory and praise of God. (Phil. 1:11)

Now may the God of peace who brought up our Lord Jesus from the dead, that great Shepherd of the sheep, through the blood of the everlasting covenant, make you complete in every good work to do His will, working in you what is well pleasing in His sight, through Jesus Christ, to whom be glory forever and ever. Amen. (Heb. 13:20–21)

You also, as living stones, are being built up a spiritual house, a holy priesthood, to offer up spiritual sacrifices acceptable to God through Jesus Christ. (1 Pet. 2:5)

Through Him

All things were made through Him, and without Him nothing was made that was made. (John 1:3)

For God did not send His Son into the world to condemn the world, but that the world through Him might be saved. (John 3:17)

And by Him everyone who believes is justified from all things from which you could not be justified by the law of Moses. (Acts 13:39)

Through Him we have received grace and apostleship for obedience to the faith among all nations for His name. (Rom. 1:5)

Through whom also we have access by faith into this grace in which we stand, and rejoice in hope of the glory of God. (Rom. 5:2)

Yet in all these things we are more than conquerors through Him who loved us. (Rom. 8:37)

For of Him and through Him and to Him are all things, to whom be glory forever. Amen. (Rom. 11:36)

For through Him we both have access by one Spirit to the Father. (Eph. 2:18)

And by Him to reconcile all things to Himself, by Him, whether things on earth or things in heaven, having made peace through the blood of His cross. (Col. 1:20)

And whatever you do in word or deed, do all in the name of the Lord Jesus, giving thanks to God the Father through Him. (Col. 3:17)

Therefore He is also able to save to the uttermost those who come to God through Him, since He always lives to make intercession for them. (Heb. 7:25)

Therefore by Him let us continually offer the sacrifice of praise to God, that is, the fruit of our lips, giving thanks to His name. (Heb. 13:15)

Who through Him believe in God, who raised Him from the dead and gave Him glory, so that your faith and hope are in God. (1 Pet. 1:21)

In this the love of God was manifested toward us, that God has sent His only begotten Son into the world, that we might live through Him. (1 John 4:9)

By Whom

Yet for us there is one God, the Father, of whom are all things, and we for Him; and one Lord Jesus Christ, through whom are all things, and through whom we live. (1 Cor. 8:6)

Through Whom

Then the word of God spread, and the number of the disciples multiplied greatly in Jerusalem, and a great many of the priests were obedient to the faith. (Acts 6:7)

Not that we have dominion over your faith, but are fellow workers for your joy; for by faith you stand. (2 Cor. 1:24)

But God forbid that I should boast except in the cross of our Lord Jesus Christ, by whom the world has been crucified to me, and I to the world. (Gal. 6:14)

Has in these last days spoken to us by His Son, whom He has appointed heir of all things, through whom also He made the worlds. (Heb. 1:2)

From Whom

And not holding fast to the Head, from whom all the body, nourished and knit together by joints and ligaments, grows with the increase that is from God. (Col. 2:19)

By Himself

Christ has redeemed us from the curse of the law, having become a curse for us (for it is written, Cursed is everyone who hangs on a tree). (Gal. 3:13)

Who being the brightness of His glory and the express image of His person, and upholding all things by the word of His power, when He had by Himself purged our sins, sat down at the right hand of the Majesty on high. (Heb. 1:3)

He then would have had to suffer often since the foundation of the world; but now, once at the end of the ages, He has appeared to put away sin by the sacrifice of Himself. (Heb. 9:26)

By His Blood

Not with the blood of goats and calves, but with His own blood He entered the Most Holy Place once for all, having obtained eternal redemption. (Heb. 9:12)

Therefore, brethren, having boldness to enter the Holiest by the blood of Jesus. (Heb. 10:19)

But if we walk in the light as He is in the light, we have fellowship with one another, and the blood of Jesus Christ His Son cleanses us from all sin. (1 John 1:7)

Of Christ

Therefore, my brethren, you also have become dead to the law through the body of Christ, that you may be married to another—to Him who was raised from the dead, that we should bear fruit to God. (Rom. 7:4)

But you are not in the flesh but in the Spirit, if indeed the Spirit of God dwells in you. Now if anyone does not have the Spirit of Christ, he is not His. (Rom. 8:9)

So then faith comes by hearing, and hearing by the word of God. (Rom. 10:17)

For who has known the mind of the Lord that he may instruct Him? But we have the mind of Christ. (1 Cor. 2:16)

Do you not know that your bodies are members of Christ? Shall I then take the members of Christ and make them members of a harlot? Certainly not! (1 Cor. 6:15)

The cup of blessing which we bless, is it not the communion of the blood of Christ? The bread which we break, is it not the communion of the body of Christ? (1 Cor. 10:16)

For we are to God the fragrance of Christ among those who are being saved and among those who are perishing. (2 Cor. 2:15)

For the love of Christ compels us, because we judge thus: that if One died for all, then all died. (2 Cor. 5:14)

To know the love of Christ which passes knowledge; that you may be filled with all the fullness of God. (Eph. 3:19)

And let the peace of God rule in your hearts, to which also you were called in one body; and be thankful. (Col. 3:15)

Now may the Lord direct your hearts into the love of God and into the patience of Christ. (2 Thess. 3:5)

How much more shall the blood of Christ, who through the eternal Spirit offered Himself without spot to God, cleanse your conscience from dead works to serve the living God? (Heb. 9:14)

Therefore, since Christ suffered for us in the flesh, arm yourselves also with the same mind, for he who has suffered in the flesh has ceased from sin. (1 Pet. 4:1)

For if these things are yours and abound, you will be neither barren nor unfruitful in the knowledge of our Lord Jesus Christ. (2 Pet. 1:8)

Now he who keeps His commandments abides in Him, and He in him. And by this we know that He abides in us, by the Spirit whom He has given us. (1 John 3:24)

Whoever transgresses and does not abide in the doctrine of Christ does not have God. He who abides in the doctrine of Christ has both the Father and the Son. (2 John 1:9)

Of Him

From whom the whole body, joined and knit together by what every joint supplies, according to the effective working by which every part does its share, causes growth of the body for the edifying of itself in love. (Eph. 4:16)

From Him

This is the message which we have heard from Him and declare to you, that God is light and in Him is no darkness at all. (1 John 1:5)

But the anointing which you have received from Him abides in you, and you do not need that anyone teach you; but as the same anointing teaches you concerning all things, and is true, and is not a lie, and just as it has taught you, you will abide in Him. (1 John 2:27)

From Whom

And not holding fast to the Head, from whom all the body, nourished and knit together by joints and ligaments, grows with the increase that is from God. (Col. 2:19)

With Christ

Now if we died with Christ, we believe that we shall also live with Him. (Rom. 6:8)

I have been crucified with Christ; it is no longer I who live, but Christ lives in me; and the life which I now live in the flesh I live by faith in the Son of God, who loved me and gave Himself for me. (Gal. 2:20)

Even when we were dead in trespasses, made us alive together with Christ (by grace you have been saved). (Eph. 2:5)

Therefore, if you died with Christ from the basic principles of the world, why, as though living in the world, do you subject yourselves to regulations. (Col. 2:20)

If then you were raised with Christ, seek those things which are above, where Christ is, sitting at the right hand of God. (Col. 3:1)

For you died, and your life is hidden with Christ in God. (Col. 3:3)

With Him

> Therefore we were buried with Him through baptism into death, that just as Christ was raised from the dead by the glory of the Father, even so we also should walk in newness of life. (Rom. 6:4)

> And you, being dead in your trespasses and the uncircumcision of your flesh, He has made alive together with Him, having forgiven you all trespasses. (Col. 2:13)

Meditate on these truths. Pray them. Say them. Confess them over and over to yourself (see Joshua 1:8). The world, the devil, our feelings and flesh, and often, even our friends and family will try to get us to say anything *but* what God has said about us. If we stubbornly "hold fast to our confession of faith," the Word will become our point of reference in terms of who we are, and that Word will come to redefine how we think about ourselves (see Hebrews 10:23). Romans 12:2 speaks of this:

> And do not be conformed to this world, but be transformed by the renewing of your mind, that you may prove what is that good and acceptable and perfect will of God.

J. B. Phillips translation of this verse says, "Don't let the world around you squeeze you into its mold." We are to resist the negative flow of this world. And this is not easy. It is a struggle. Paul called it "spiritual warfare" in 2 Corinthians 10:3–5. And one of the primary ways we can win this war is by aligning our words with God's Word. It is impossible for us to successfully fight thoughts with thoughts. It is very difficult to think one thing and speak another. We have to use words. Negative, fear-filled thoughts can only be defeated with positive, faith-filled words. Speaking faith-filled words is one of the most effective weapons in our arsenal. One writer said that language "molds one's whole outlook on life." He continued, "Thinking follows the tracks laid down in one's language" ("How Language Shapes Our Thoughts," Stewart Chase, *Harper's Magazine*, April, 1954). I love that!

As you meditate on God's Word and relentlessly align your words with His, your thoughts will line up with His thoughts, also (see Isaiah 55:8–9). Then you will begin to discover the specifics, the nuances of your own individual calling. Valerie and I's I Am Statement grew as we talked and walked in agreement with the written Word. I have recited many of those verses in the list I just shared hundreds of times over the past thirty years. With that in mind, pay attention to our current personal I Am Statement again:

> I am a successful pastor of a powerful and growing church. I lead with wisdom, excellence, boldness and confidence.
>
> I am a man of tremendous influence. I have favor with God, favor with man, and I am feared in hell.
>
> I plant and water with joy and faith knowing God is giving the increase and I am anxious for nothing.

> I am a ridiculous giver. I am known for my generosity and I am a blessing to the Body of Christ worldwide.
>
> Debts are eliminated, reserves are generated, and LifePoint is a financial powerhouse with more than enough to do all God has have called us to do.
>
> People are looking at us and saying, "Of all people, I never thought it would be you who is so blessed!"

Notice, our I Am Statement is in agreement with what the written Word says, but it is also specifically tailored to Valerie and me—to what we believe God has spoken to us personally.

Maybe God called you to be an entrepreneur or an engineer. Maybe He's called you to be a stay-at-home parent and homeschool your children. Maybe you are called to be a veterinarian or a welder or an artist or a church planter. Maybe God called you to teach in a university or serve God in another country—or something entirely different or any combination of these. The details about God's specific word for your life will become more and more clear as you get ahold of and align to the general truths of God's written word. You should be relentless. Confess His word over you and refuse to deviate—come hell or high water. As you begin to see yourself as He sees you, take that vision and put it into a statement, a format that you can memorize and recite daily. That is your I Am Statement. If you will do this, your life will dramatically change—for the good.

Now, you need to understand that you may be criticized for putting these principles into practice. Some religious folks even hold these concepts in contempt. They label them in a pejorative sense: "name it and claim it" or "easy believism." And granted, there have been abuses when taken to an extreme (as can be the case with any doctrine). However, it has been my experience that *there is nothing easy about lining one's words up with God's Word*. It is like swimming upstream. It is spiritual warfare. But extraordinary results require extraordinary sacrifice. And controlling our words is a profound sacrifice. But you must understand, it is only one in a series of many more. The road to finding your higher self is paved with the continual sacrifice of your lower self, with all of its carnal baggage we are prone to accumulate. Proverbs 23:23 (KJV) says, "Buy the truth and sell it not." Your old self is the currency used to "buy" your new, true self. In other words, your true self is quite expensive because it is hard for us to let go of our old self. That is why the old self must be crucified—literally nailed to a tree. The truth is, if we are to walk with the Lord, the level of sacrifice never decreases. As a matter of fact, it actually increases. Abraham profoundly blazed this trail for us, as well.

Notice, not only did God require Abraham to consistently control the way he talked about himself, but God immediately asked him to circumcise himself. This has profound spiritual implications, but suffice it to say that to Abraham, this was a flesh and blood sacrifice. God's request was audacious but Abraham's response was even more so. Shockingly, he immediately complied. This is remarkable. And then, Abraham turned around and talked over three hundred of his men into doing the same thing. You can just hear those ol' fellas now—"Um, you say the Voice has been talking to you again, huh? And He told *you...what?*" And then Abraham sold them on it! Talk about leadership!

Here is the point: The initial result of Abraham calling himself precisely what God had called him unlocked a willingness to radically obey no matter the cost. And this kind of radical obedience was contagious. He was able to inspire others to the same level of commitment. Abraham's complete compliance and total obedience was absolutely necessary for Isaac's birth. But to get to that point, he had to begin with his words. Again, this not just "say it and have it." But saying it led to a level of obedience that Abraham had never experienced before. And once he broke through to this level of sacrifice, there was no going back. He had discovered his true self. He had lost the low life and found the high life. So much so that years later, on Mount Moriah, God asked Abraham for the ultimate sacrifice, his son, and he did not hesitate (Genesis 22). But it all started with his stubborn and relentless insistence of calling himself exactly what God had called him: "I am who I Am says I am!"

Failing Forward

*You may encounter many defeats, but you must not be defeated.
In fact, it may be necessary to encounter the defeats,
so you can know who you are, what you can rise from,
how you can still come out of it.*
—Maya Angelou

If you are a follower of Jesus, then the Bible calls you "Abraham's seed" (Gal. 3:29). The reality is, just as the *father* of the faithful made plenty of mistakes, so do his children. Often what we call a "mistake," the Bible calls "sin." The Hebrew and Greek words for sin mean "to miss the mark." In the book of Romans, we learn that "whatever is not of faith is sin" and that "faith comes by hearing…the Word of God" (Rom. 14:23; 10:17). So, when we behave in a way that is contrary to the Word, we are, in effect, sinning. It is the will of God for us *not* to sin, but with the Word's strict definition of what sin is, the truth is you and I will commit our share of sins on our faith journey. As a matter of fact, I have never met anyone who did not.

Many years ago, I worked alongside a very outspoken self-proclaimed Christian. One day, he shocked me when he looked me in the eyes and with a straight face said, "Since I became a Christian fourteen years ago, I have not committed one sin!"

I smirked and waited for the punch line. My response seemed to agitate him, so he doubled down. "I'm serious, Donavon." His voice was cracking with conviction.

As the truth began to dawn on me, I thought, *This guy is convinced that he is perfect!*

I mustered all the sincerity and compassion I could, looked him back in the eyes and unflinchingly said, "You… are…a…liar! You just sinned by telling me that!"

That did not go over too well. But I was so shocked by the audacity of this guy that I felt I *had* to call him out on his ridiculous and foolish claim. You see, we had spent many hours, days, and weeks together. We had even gotten our families together a few times. I heard things he said. I saw things he did. He was an overall good guy, but he had a bad temper, among other issues.

I called him out on his hypocrisy, but to my surprise, he had an answer for everything I said, both philosophically and theologically. When I told him he had an anger "problem," he said, "Well, I never let the sun go down on my wrath." I was dumbfounded.

I reasoned with him, "Do you think it's a sin to not tithe?"

He said, "Absolutely."

I continued, "So on your very first paycheck after you got saved, did you tithe?"

Stunningly, he responded, "Brother, I was tithing *before* I got saved!"

I belly-laughed and said, "Dude, you're impossible!"

Over the next few days, I picked his brain—not to change his mind—but to figure out what made him tick. I did a forensic investigation of his underlying rationale in an attempt to discover what would cause this guy to actually think that he had never sinned since he got saved. Eventually, he admitted to me that he had "made mistakes," but he said that was different. His argument was one of semantics. So trust me when I say, everybody makes mistakes, missteps, and yes, even sins in their walk with God—even *this* guy! And Abraham was no different.

Partial Obedience?

Now, remember, God called Abraham to leave Ur—the place—and to leave Ur—the people—even his family. Abram left Ur, all right, but he dragged his family with him. The fact that Abram left his land but not his clan could be considered, at best, "partial obedience." Right? He obeyed only part of what God had told him. Now, I have heard it said that "partial obedience is disobedience," and I get it. I certainly push myself, and encourage the people I lead and influence to fully obey whatever God has said. But the truth is, we often obey in percentages. Full surrender takes time. Full surrender requires process.

So how does God see our partial steps in the right direction? Notice what Hebrews 11:8 says about Abram's first steps. "By faith Abraham obeyed when he was called to go out to the place which he would receive as an inheritance. And he went out, not knowing where he was going." The hall-of-fame of faith, Hebrews 11, does not even mention the fact that he dragged his family along. Terah, Haran, and Lot—none of them are mentioned in this summation. They are not even alluded to or hinted at. It does *not* say, "By faith Abram *partially* obeyed." It just says, "By faith [he] obeyed." His obedience, the part about leaving his land, the part he got right, is the only part that counted in the eyes of God at the time. I love that!

Now, do not think that his full obedience did not matter, because it did. Abram would learn that lesson soon enough. God predicated the fulfillment of the promises on Abram's faithful and full obedience. Again, notice verse 1 of Genesis 12, "Get out of your country, from your family and from your father's house, to a land that I will show you." And then, "I will bless you and make your name great." But in Abram's newfound faith, God did not slam him for the part he got wrong; rather, he celebrated him for the part he got right. Is that not awesome?

Can I tell you something? God will not write you off because of the part of the Word that you have yet to obey; rather, he will rejoice with you over the part you *have* obeyed. God looks at what you got right. God looks at what you *have* surrendered. And He says, "That's good! I can work with that! You keep walking!"

Please do not get so high and mighty that you think God just dismisses people who have not all-the-way obeyed everything He has told them. If God did that, none of us could survive.

Lamentations 3:22–23 says,

> *Through* the Lord's mercies we are not consumed, because His compassions fail not. *They are* new every morning; Great *is* Your faithfulness.

Are you grateful for his mercy? I know I am.

Abram was a new convert. He had never followed God before. Nobody in his family had ever followed God. They were all idolaters. He had no mentor. His heart was like a garden full of weeds. God had to recultivate and repurpose it in order to turn it into a field of fruitfulness. It would take time for Abram's obedience to expand and for his courage and faith to grow. Progress would be slow. It would take years, but eventually, he would yield more and more areas of his heart to the plan of God. God was changing his heart from a heart of idolatry to a heart of worship for the true and living God. It was a process—a *slow* process. We are talking crockpot, not microwave.

And part of the reason why the process was slow was because he was dragging around the dead weight of his father's household—Terah, Haran, Lot, et al. It is hard to run in a way that will cause you to win if you are carrying around big weights. Imagine trying to run a marathon while dragging a giant truck tire. That is what CrossFit folks do, not marathon runners. No wonder the writer of Hebrews says, "Therefore we also, since we are surrounded by so great a cloud of witnesses, let us lay aside every weight, and the sin which so easily ensnares *us,* and let us run with endurance the race that is set before us" (Heb. 12:1).

It is interesting to notice that the runner in this passage is still in the race even though he is weighted down. Even with the weight, he is encouraged to run. Ecclesiastes 9:11 says, "The race is not to the swift." The idea is this, we are to run until we cross the finish line. In Matthew 24:13, Jesus said, "He that endures to the end shall be saved."

The question is not, "How fast are you running?" The question is, "Are you still in the race?" It is not, "How far along are you?" It is, "Which way are you facing? Are you still moving forward?"

You may be inching along. That is OK. You are still in the race. You may even be stuck, temporarily standing still. That is OK, too. Just make sure you are facing the right direction. As a pastor, I tell people all the time, if, at this time, you cannot take a step in the right direction, just lean in the right direction. That is better than doing nothing.

For years, Abram lived halfway between Ur and Canaan. As a matter of fact, he did not live in the land where God had called him. He had no kid, no nation, no worldwide impact. He had come up short of the blessings and short of the promises. During this season, you could look at Abram and say, "It doesn't look like your dreams will *ever* come true. It doesn't look like you'll *ever* get what God promised you."

He had hit a wall. He had stalled out. He looked like a total failure. But here's what I love about Abram, he kept leaning into the promises—"You promised me greatness, blessing, and multiplication, and I'm not settling for less!" He knew he was destined for more, even though the sum of his current experience did not equal what God had promised. He refused to be defined by his current status, by his delays, by his failures, by his losses. Rather, he chose to be defined by the promises of God.

So often, we think we are the only one who ever gets stuck in a moment, hits a wall, stalls out, fails, or loses. We tend to think, *Well, I guess that's just how I am. I always miss it. I always fail. I'm a failure. I'm just not like brother super Christian over here.* I want you to know, every hero of the faith got stuck at some time, failed at some time, dropped the ball at some time. You are not alone.

Ask Adam.
Ask Eve.
Ask Noah.
Ask David.
Ask Elijah.
Ask Jonah.
Ask Peter.

We have already looked at some of the parallels with Abraham and Peter. And in the area of personal failure, there are no greater parallels. Both Abraham and Peter failed miserably. But they did not let those delays, missteps, mistakes, sins, losses, and failures define them. We can learn a lot from these heroes of the faith. Do not let a bad season, a lapse in judgment, or a failure of any kind define you. Even if it is your own fault, even if it is because you partially obeyed, you have to let faith rise up and say, "I may have partially obeyed, I may have gotten stuck halfway, I may have wasted a lot of time and made a mountain of mistakes, but my story's not over. This is not the end of my story. This is just a chapter, and I'm turning the page. I'm writing a new chapter."

In the face of failure and loss, faith rises like a phoenix out of the ashes and rubble and says, "I am who I Am says I am. I can have what I Am says I can have. I can do what I Am says I can do. I still have a dream, and I'm not quitting until I see it come to pass." Isaiah 61:3 says our God will give us "beauty for ashes…the oil of joy for mourning," and establish us like trees of righteousness." Joel 2:25 says He will "restore the years the locust and cankerworm have eaten." You need to know this: your best days are not behind you. Your story is not over.

Hey, Abram, your destiny is written in the stars.

Hey, Rahab, your destiny is in your willingness to pivot.

Hey, Samson, your destiny is as close as that growing hair on your head.

Hey, Gideon, your destiny is in your willingness to just do something.

Hey, Bathsheba, your destiny is in your willingness to forgive and accept forgiveness.

Hey, woman at the well, your destiny is in the One who shows up when least expected.

Hey, woman caught in the act of adultery, He's writing your destiny in the sand.

Our beloved Jesus is a savior, a redeemer, Who has already written the next chapter of your life. Those dreams He put in your heart are still there, waiting for you to get up and move on.

Abram finally did move on. He spent some time in Egypt, where, out of fear, he lied "like a rug." He told the king that Sarai was his sister, so the king took her into his harem. That was almost a disaster. It is not like Abram was malicious, rather, he was a street-wise survivor doing all he knew to do to stay alive, to the point of compromising his integrity. But did God throw Abram away? No. As a matter of fact, God bailed him out. He gave Abimilech a dream and, in the dream, warned him not to touch Sarai. God protected Sarai, Abram, Abimilech, and His own Word, *in spite of* Abram's lack of integrity. God worked around Abram's mistakes and missteps because God was determined to see His Word come to pass in Abram's life.

You may have compromised your integrity at times because you were afraid, you were doing what you felt like you had to do to survive. That certainly doesn't make it right, but I'm here to tell you, God is determined to see the Word He's spoken over you come to pass in your life. He "*watches over His Word to perform it*" (Jer. 1:12). Numbers 23:19 says, God is "*not a man that He should lie*." *We* may lie, but God never does.

Understand, your story is not over. There is a chapter beyond your worst failure. There is a chapter beyond your seasons of fear and compromise. I love the fact that, through the good times and the bad times, Abram held on to his dream. It was who he was at an atomic level. He was constantly asking God, every time he got a chance, "What about my dream?"

I AM[3]

What About Your Dream

Wilma Rudolph was the twentieth of twenty-two children. She was born prematurely on June 23, 1940, in St. Bethlehem, Tennessee. She weighed just four-and-a-half pounds. The bulk of her childhood was spent in bed. She suffered from double pneumonia, scarlet fever, and later she contracted polio. After losing the use of her left leg, she was fitted with a metal leg brace when she was six. At the age of nine, she removed the brace and began to walk without it. By the age of thirteen, she had developed a rhythmic walk, which doctors said was something of a miracle. That same year, she decided she wanted to become a runner. She entered a race and came in last place.

For the next few years every race she entered, she came in last. Everyone told her to quit, but she kept on running. One day, she actually won a race. Then she won another one and continued winning races. Eventually, this little girl, who was told she would never walk again, went on to compete in the Olympics. At the 1960 Rome Olympics, she won the hundred-meter race against the fleet-footed German Yetta Heine, who was considered to be the fastest woman in the world. She beat her again in the two hundred-meter race. Next, as the anchor for the US team in the four hundred-meter-relay race, Rudolph dropped the baton. This gave Heine, the anchor for the German team, the break she needed. But it was not meant to be. Wilma Rudolph had a dream that defined her at an atomic level. Like she had done so many times before, Wilma overcame her disadvantage, overcame Heine, and won the four hundred-meter. At the age of twenty, the little premature girl who had suffered with polio and had worn a leg brace, shattered world records, and became known "the fastest woman in the world." She was the first American woman to win three gold medals in one Olympics. Wilma Rudolph once said, "My mother taught me very early to believe I could achieve any accomplishment I wanted to. The first was to walk without braces."

Interestingly and perhaps ironically, "Wilma" means *desire* and "Rudolph" means *fame and glory*. Wilma Rudolph had a dream deep at her core, at an atomic level. So what about your dream?

Praying Your I Am Statement in the Spirit

You say I am loved when I can't feel a thing
You say I am strong when I think I am weak
And you say I am held when I am falling short
And when I don't belong, oh You say I am Yours
And I believe oh I believe
What You say of me
I believe.

—Lauren Daigle

The Holy Spirit wants to help you pray your "I Am Statement." If you already pray in tongues, then you have already been praying your "I Am Statement" without even realizing it (albeit with His help). Some may be wondering, "What in the world are you talking about, Donavon?" Let me explain.

When I use the term, "speaking in tongues," I mean "speaking in a language you do not naturally know, as the Holy Spirit enables you to do so." Speaking in tongues is not something that died with the last apostle or the last person that they "empowered" to do so. Speaking in tongues is for us *now*, in the twenty-first century. In the New Covenant, everyone who turns to Jesus has the privilege of praying in the Spirit, or praying in tongues. When you are initially filled with the Holy Spirit, you speak in tongues, just like they did in the book of Acts. This is called the doctrine of *initial evidence*. But it does not stop there. Now you have a supernatural partner to help you pray the will of God into existence throughout your Christian journey, and one of the ways you will do so is by praying in tongues.

To some, this sounds just too fantastic and mystical for Christianity. But let me remind you, as Christians, we say we believe in a God who cannot be seen, who created everything that we can see—the material world—with just His Word. That is pretty fantastic and mystical, right? One of the problems with modern Christianity is that, in our walk with God, we have become too far removed from the supernatural and extraordinary. Such was not the case in the church that Apostle Paul planted in Corinth. As a matter of fact, in his first letter to the Corinthians, he devoted two entire chapters to the subject of governing the fantastic, grand and glorious gifts of the Spirit, as they were "out of control." True story (see chapters 12 and 14 of 1 Corinthians).

Now, 1 Corinthians 12:28 (NIV) says there are "different kinds of [speaking in] tongues." There are at least three different kinds of speaking in tongues. There is tongues as the *initial evidence* that one has been baptized in the Holy Ghost (Acts 2:37, Acts 10:22, Acts 19:23). Then, there is the *gift of tongues*, which is meant to be interpreted (1 Corinthians 12 and 14). Lastly, there is *praying in tongues,* or as it has been popularly called within the charismatic movement, one's *prayer language* (Jude 1:20).

It has been my observation throughout many years of speaking in tongues, as well as ministering throughout the Pentecostal movement, and some within the charismatic movement and other Spirit-filled circles, that people who speak in tongues regularly, do so with a particular cadence, syntax, dialect, and accent. As a matter of fact, these patterns can even become engrained into one's memory. If you speak in tongues consistently in your Christian walk, then you know what I am talking about, and you are familiar with your own unique flow and the patterns in which you pray in the Spirit. However, if I am used in the "gift of tongues," which is to be interpreted, then those tongues can be somewhat different than my "normal" praying in the Spirit. Because I was so young, I do not recall the specifics of when I was first filled with the Holy Ghost and how it sounded when I first spoke in tongues, but I suspect it was a primitive version of the prayer language, in which I now pray every day.

This has become quite fascinating to me. I have heard many friends and mentors speak in tongues, and they say similar phrases every time I hear them. As a matter of fact, I can mimic them, if I so choose. Critics say this tongue-talking stuff is ridiculous and just a bunch of mumbo-jumbo or gibberish. But I have become convinced that what is happening when you are praying in your prayer language, or praying in the Spirit, is that you are praying God's calling and destiny over your life. The Holy Spirit is impressing, inspiring, and enabling you to pray your "I Am Statement," which in turn, is calling it to come to pass in your life.

First Corinthians 12:3 in the New International Version of the Bible states, "He that speaks in an unknown tongue speaks mysteries." Those "mysteries" are things you do not understand, but they are the will of God. You cannot pray any more in the will of God than when you are praying in the Spirit. And 1 John 5:14 says that if we ask anything "according to His will," He hears us and grants us what we have asked. The famous verse, Romans 8:28, which says, "And we know that all things work together for good to those who love God, to those who are the called according to His purpose" is directly linked to the previous two verses. Notice:

> Likewise the Spirit also helps in our weaknesses. For we do not know what we should pray for as we ought, but the Spirit Himself makes intercession for us with groanings which cannot be uttered. Now He who searches the hearts knows what the mind of the Spirit is, because He makes intercession for the saints according to the will of God.

The good that is worked out *is* worked out through praying in the Spirit, or by praying in unintelligible speech, or in tongues.

I was raised in a Pentecostal church, received the Holy Spirit at the age of seven, and spoke in tongues throughout my childhood and teenage years. However, when I was a young adult, I hit a bump in the road. Through a series of tragic events, which included the moral failure of a mentor and resulting church trouble, I chose to walk another path, which was a dreadful mistake. But let me take you back to something that happened to me when I was fifteen years old.

I had come home from a corporate prayer meeting where I had been seeking the will of God for my life. For several weeks, I had been feeling as though I would spend my life either preaching or being involved in some sort of music ministry for the Lord. I was smart enough to realize that if I could discover which of these was His precise direction, then I could begin focusing on that one and make my subsequent decisions based on His perfect will, including which college to attend, and on and on. At that particular prayer meeting,

I really did not get any kind of clear direction, but afterward, I went home; and while in my room, I began to pray. Then, I began to thumb through my Bible and came across Romans 10:14, which says, "*How then shall they call on Him in whom they have not believed? And how shall they believe in Him of whom they have not heard? And how shall they hear without a preacher?*"

As I read these words, I heard the Lord speak to me on the inside. "*Donavon, put preaching first and your music will always compliment your preaching ministry.*" I was young, naive, and had come across this verse in a way that sounds like Bible roulette, but I had no doubt: I had heard the voice of God. I had found the will of God for my life. I knew the direction in which I should move. And I did so with all my might.

Just a few years later, while I was attending Bible school, pursuing His will to the best of my ability, the disaster I mentioned earlier took place. As the weeks and months dragged on, and the collateral damage intensified, I became discouraged and despondent. At this low time in my life, I put preaching on the backburner and decided to pursue a music career in Nashville, Tennessee. I had some connections there, and exploited them to the fullest. With my life assignment out of order, I moved to Nashville, and very quickly, began to lose perspective. I quit going to church, questioned everything, and the anger I had experienced over losing a mentor and the subsequent fallout, turned to bitterness. I went from bad to worse. I threw out godly standards by which I had lived my life, while still trying to hold on to the basic tenets of my faith. Then, I began to lose my grip on the fundamentals. It was not long before I viewed Christianity as just another world religion. Nothing more. Nothing less. I am leaving out many of the details of my disillusionment, but the bottom line is this, the fifteen-year-old kid from Bossier City, Louisiana, had clearly lost his way.

A few years later, however, I found myself restless and longing for the peace I had experienced as a younger man. While I would have never admitted it, I was indeed a prodigal, and as a prodigal, I had memories of my time in the Father's house. (See Luke 15:11–32.) I was homesick. I was searching for the place where I belonged, and I began to wonder if, perhaps, it was that place out of which I had stormed so long ago. Now, to be sure, there were a lot of people praying for me—my new wife, my family, and my countless friends. And thank God for their prayers. Then, *I* began to pray.

I started praying prayers like this,

> God, if you are real, then I would like the feeling of peace and belonging that I had as a kid. I know I've discounted all of those feelings as hypnosis and group-think, but if it is real, then I want it back.

I began to listen to recordings of old sermons that had moved me when I was younger, and I even began to fast. That was huge. I hated fasting then, and I hate it now. But with all that, I did not find what I was looking for.

When I was younger, I used to "feel" the presence of the Lord. It was a sanctuary of peace, belonging, clarity, cleansing, and wholeness. At times, I would cry in His presence. At times, I would laugh. But I was always *home* in His presence. When I got older and jaded, however, I explained away the euphoria of His presence. "It's just conditioning, mind control, goosebumps, Pentecostal brainwashing," I would say.

But now, I was not so sure. I was opening up. I *wanted* those feelings that came from *feeling* His presence.

Finally, one day on my lunchbreak, I came home to our little house in Shreveport, Louisiana, and in sincere desperation, I fell across my bed and began to pray. But this time, it was different. I said,

> Lord, when I was young, I used to speak in tongues. I haven't done anything like that for years, but I remember how it sounded when I used to do so. Now I know this sounds silly, but I am going to say those words and phrases like I used to and, if You're real, would You please help me break through into Your presence?

I had the sense that I was standing on a cliff and it was time to jump. So I did. While "feeling" nothing, I *started to start* saying those words and phrases from my memory. But as I did, as I gave voice to the very first syllable, *immediately*, I was overwhelmed by the Holy Spirit! *That was the first time I had felt His presence in years!* The Father had run to me and He embraced me! I was home! And it was in that moment that He spoke to me, quoting John 12:24, "'Except a corn of wheat fall into the ground and die, it abides alone, but if it falls into the ground and dies, it bears much fruit.' Donavon, everything you've held on to, your thoughts, your ideas, your plans, your dreams, they all have to die!" He was reminding me to realign my life to His plans and purposes to that initial order of "put your preaching ministry first and your music will always compliment that."

That was a life-altering breakthrough. I had felt His presence. I had heard His voice. I was a puddle of tears, completely wrecked, wholly undone, fully surrendered and happier than I had been in years. I was back in the Father's house. As I prayed in the Spirit, it sounded just like it did when I was a younger man. Why? Because the Holy Spirit was helping me pray the will of God over my life as He had done years before. His will had never changed. My calling was the same. Since that day, I have prayed in tongues almost every day, and I am living out the dreams God put in my heart when I was just a fifteen-year-old kid sitting on the side of my bed in Bossier City, Louisiana.

In Chapter 1, we looked at the name change Apostle Paul experienced in Acts 13. I find it interesting that in 1 Corinthians 14:18, Paul said, "I thank God I speak with tongues more than you all." Could it be that his destiny was connected to his praying in the Spirit? And Peter, who also had a name change in Matthew 16, prayed in the Spirit post-Pentecost in Acts 4:31. Notice: "And when they had prayed, the place where they were assembled together was shaken; and they were all filled with the Holy Spirit, and they spoke the word of God with boldness." Again, was his destiny tied to his prayer language? I believe that is the case.

We can certainly see from Acts 8:4–24 that Peter saw the necessity of all who turned to Jesus being filled with the Spirit and speaking in tongues initially. When Philip went to Samaria and preached Christ, many were delivered and baptized in water, but they had not been filled with the Holy Ghost. Samaritans were delivered from demons, baptized in water and filled with joy, but not the Holy Spirit. How did Philip know they had not been filled? How did the apostles at Jerusalem know they had not been filled? I believe it was because these folks had not spoken in tongues.

Lest we see this as a justification for *not* speaking in tongues, notice what the apostles immediately did. They cleared their incredibly busy calendars and sent Peter and John to jump-start the Samaritans' experience in the Spirit. While the text does not say explicitly that the Samaritans spoke with tongues, the implicit evidence points to a sign, something that signaled them having been filled, some evidence that let Peter, John, and Philip know when these Samaritans had indeed been filled with the Holy Spirit. And upon receiving this Spirit baptism, the Samaritans had the opportunity—the privilege—to pray in the Spirit, thus tapping into and unleashing the atomic power of who they were in Christ.

Let me ask you, do you pray in tongues? If not, begin to ask the Lord to help you find that place of comfort and power. You have a destiny and a calling. My prayer is that you will find it, pray it and fulfill it—to the glory of God.

Remembering the Future

*Remember the former things of old, for I am God,
and there is no other; I am God, and there is none like Me,
Declaring the end from the beginning, and from ancient times
things that are not yet done, saying, "My counsel shall stand,
And I will do all My pleasure."*
—Isaiah 46:9–10

E. L. and Nona Freeman served as missionaries to South Africa for over forty-one years. Nona tells the fascinating story of one of their early converts, Teklemariam Gezahagne, who was travelling and preaching throughout the Wollo Province in Ethiopia. Tekle, as he was affectionately known, was resting under a large tree just outside of a village, when he simply broke a small branch off the tree. Soon, he noticed a crowd from the village approaching him. Tekle thought the Lord was sending him an audience to hear the Word. Then he noticed the axes, knives, spears, and angry faces.

What Tekle did not know was that, to these villagers, this particular tree was considered to be a god and had been venerated for generations. Priests would ritualistically sprinkle the tree with butter and blood. To them, it was sacred, and Tekle had just desecrated their beloved tree. Tekle had to think fast, and apparently, the Lord helped restrain the crowd long enough for him to make his case. Freeman relates the story.

He asked them, "Which one do you think is bigger." Tekle pointed, "This tree or the mountain yonder?"

They looked at the mountain thoughtfully and replied, "The mountain is larger."

"Now, tell me," Tekle asked, "is the mountain or the heaven bigger?"

All of them gazed at the sky and answered, "It must be the heaven."

Praying silently, Tekle phrased the most important question of all. "Is the heaven or the creator of the heaven bigger?"

Everyone fell silent. The scowls had vanished. Finally an old man said, "The one who created the heaven must be the greatest of all."

Tekle exclaimed with a happy smile, "I worship this big creator of the heaven and the earth, and I have come to tell you about Him" (Freeman, Nona, 1987, *Unseen Hands, The Story of Revival in Ethiopia*, p. 37, Word of Flame).

I love that story. It simply illustrates the bigness of God. The creator is far superior to that which he creates. Therefore, as His creation, we are to worship Him. If we worship anything created, we are worshiping that which is far inferior. This is foolishness and leads to darkness. (See Romans 1:25.)

Just how big is our God? Nothing reveals His bigness quite like His relationship to time. God created time, and space, for that matter (pun intended). In science, space and time are often referenced together and called spacetime. As the creator of spacetime, our God is not limited by it. He transcends it. He is, after all, the God of the "omnis"—*omniscient*, *omnipotent*, and *omnipresent*, meaning, He is all-knowing, all-powerful, and everywhere at the same "time."

I AM[3]

Isaiah 46:10 says that God "declare[s] the end from the beginning." He is not restricted to or confined by spacetime. He does not necessarily view time as linear or sequential. It seems as if God sees the past, present, and future simultaneously, as an eternal now, which is mindboggling. We struggle to wrap our minds around this. Paul said we see through a glass darkly, and Isaiah said His thoughts are higher than ours, so we have to squint and intensify our gaze as we look higher, deeper, and unconventionally into the mysteries of God (see 1 Corinthians 13:12 and Isaiah 55:8–9).

Theologians refer specifically to the foreknowledge God as His *prescience*. He knows things in advance, ahead of "time." God starts with the *end* in mind—that is to say, the *outcome*, the desired *result*, and in a sense, reverse engineers everything required in order to make that result occur. He programs a process whereby the outcome, His will, is inevitable. That is how big our God is!

The story of Joseph testifies to the prescience of God and His remarkable ability to engineer His will into the process. Joseph was the son of Jacob and Rachel. He was a dreamer, and who God had called him to be was programmed into his spiritual DNA. It went even deeper, to an atomic level. Who he really *was* was hardwired into the core of his makeup. He was preloaded with potential world-changing power. His dreams were of blessing and greatness, to the extent that he saw his father and brothers bowing before him. His dreams were grand that they even made Jacob shake his head in doubt, and he *adored* Joseph and showered him with gifts. Between the dreams and the favor of his father, Joseph's brothers were driven mad with jealousy. Finally, their rage drove them to toss him into a pit and leave him to die while they picnicked at the pit's edge to celebrate his demise. Just because you have God-dreams does not mean everybody is going to rejoice with you.

Then his brothers pulled him from the pit only to sell him to slave traders and pocket a few shekels. Upon entering Egypt, Joseph was "bought" by Potipher, whom he served faithfully, bringing unprecedented prosperity to his house. All was fine and dandy until Joseph rebuffed the advances of Mrs. Potipher. She falsely accused him of inappropriate behavior, and he was promptly placed in prison. Chances are, Potipher did not believe his wife or he would have had Joseph immediately executed. While in prison, Joseph rose to become the head trustee and helped other dreamers, the baker and the butler, by interpreting their dreams.

The baker was executed and the butler was restored, just as Joseph had said it would happen. Joseph asked the butler to put in a good word to Pharaoh because he was there on a trumped-up charge. But the butler did not until a couple of years later when Pharaoh himself started dreaming. Finally, in *one day*, Joseph was promoted from the prison to the palace.

Years later, when food was amply available in Egypt and the rest of the world was starving, just as Pharaoh's dreams had predicted, Joseph's brothers came to Egypt to get food. Joseph recognized them in the crowd but they did not recognize him. He looked like an Egyptian and spoke the Egyptian language. As far as his brothers were concerned, Joseph was just some Egyptian who was Pharaoh's right-hand man. Joseph met with them and spoke to them through an interpreter. He began to test his brothers to see if they had changed and matured. After a clever battery of these tests, Joseph realized his brothers were willing to lay down their lives for their younger brother, Benjamin, whom he had just met. They had indeed changed, so he asked the Egyptians to leave the room and he began to speak to them in Hebrew, revealing himself to them. The entire household of Jacob relocated to Egypt, and yes, they all bowed before Joseph. Joseph not only saved his family, he ended up saving the world during this desperate time.

Years later, Jacob died. Upon his death, Joseph's brothers became worried that Joseph might turn on them and seek revenge. Then, in Genesis 50:19-21, Joseph delivered his swansong, making his intentions clear. Notice the astonishing assertion Joseph makes concerning the prescience of God:

> Joseph said to them, "Do not be afraid, for am I in the place of God? But as for you, you meant evil against me; but God meant it for good, in order to bring it about as it is this day, to save many people alive. Now therefore, do not be afraid; I will provide for you and your little ones." And he comforted them and spoke kindly to them.

God had reverse-engineered the process. Why were the Midianites passing by at the precise moment Joseph's brothers were having the pit-side picnic? Why did Potipher, of all people, buy Joseph? Why *that* prison? Why were Pharaoh's butler and baker in *that* prison at *that* time? And that is just scratching the surface of the questions we could ask. Suffice it to say, Our God is a big God! And by the way, the jealousy of his brothers was not part of Joseph's dream. As a matter of fact, he only saw them bowing. The pit was not in Joseph's dream. Neither was the prison. But all of those things were part of the *process* that positioned Joseph for the fulfillment of his dream.

Beautiful in Time

God has a plan *for time* that has been conceived *in eternity*. That is why His plans can seem so "out of time" to us. In Ecclesiastes 3:11, Solomon made this observation: "He has made everything beautiful in its time. Also He has put eternity in their hearts, except that no one can find out the work that God does from beginning to end." The dream in your heart is born in eternity. However, that dreams worked out *in time*—from beginning to end. In the pursuit of it, you will experience things that you did not see in the dream. Understand, if you did not see it in the dream, it is part of the process. It is the means to the end. And none of what you are experiencing is a surprise to God. Keep your attitude right, never lose sight of the dream, and even help others with their dreams along the way. Yield to the process, and one day, you will wake up living in your dream. Numbers 23:19 tells us that "God is not a man that He should lie." Jeremiah 1:12 (KJV) says God "watches over His word to perform it." There is a certainty when it comes to His word and His will. Keep believing, and in time, you will see the beauty of His plan.

The second Psalm speaks of His prescience and the certainty of His will. Notice,

> Why do the nations rage, and the people plot a vain thing? The kings of the earth set themselves, and the rulers take counsel together, against the LORD and against His Anointed, saying, "Let

> us break Their bonds in pieces and cast away Their cords from us." He who sits in the heavens shall laugh; the LORD shall hold them in derision. Then He shall speak to them in His wrath, and distress them in His deep displeasure: "Yet I have set My King on My holy hill of Zion. I will declare the decree: The LORD has said to Me, 'You are My Son, today I have begotten You. Ask of Me, and I will give You the nations for Your inheritance, and the ends of the earth for Your possession. You shall break them with a rod of iron; You shall dash them to pieces like a potter's vessel.'" Now therefore, be wise, O kings; be instructed, you judges of the earth. Serve the LORD with fear, and rejoice with trembling. Kiss the Son, lest He be angry, and you perish in the way, when His wrath is kindled but a little. Blessed are all those who put their trust in Him.

The Lord is saying that all of hell could not stop His redemptive plans and purposes. The best thing any of us can do is to embrace His plans and purposes, and they are all wrapped up in "the Son," that is in Jesus. So where do you fit in to His plans? What is your place in His prophetic purposes? Ask yourself, *Who does I Am say I am?* and *What does I Am say I am to do?*

Understand, there is intricate programing that has gone into you, your circumstances, your life. There is a calling that has been hardwired into you from the very beginning. Notice the words of David in Psalm 139:13–16,

> For You formed my inward parts; You covered me in my mother's womb. I will praise You, for I am fearfully and wonderfully made; marvelous are Your works, and that my soul knows very well. My frame was not hidden from You, when I was made in secret, and skillfully wrought in the lowest parts of the earth. Your eyes saw my substance, being yet unformed. And in Your book they all were written, the days fashioned for me, when as yet there were none of them.

The fact that David would slay Goliath was hardwired into David prenatally. It was in his spiritual DNA. It was in him at an atomic level. Could he have sabotaged that calling? Certainly. But he chose to live a life surrendered to God and to God's calling. He chose to live from the inside out. When he was defending his father's sheep in the middle of nowhere, killing lions and bears, God was preparing him for an encounter in the Valley of Elah with a giant named Goliath. Did David know it at the time? Not at all. But by simply putting God first, even in the littlest ways, like by helping protect his father's property, David was inadvertently aligning himself with his destiny. I believe there was an "itch" in his spirit, and he was doing all he knew at the time to scratch it. Eventually, the endgame was revealed, his explosive destiny was detonated, and the rest is history. It works the same with you and me.

Notice what the Lord tells Jeremiah the first chapter of the book that bears his name, verses 4 and 5,

> Then the word of the LORD came to me, saying: "Before I formed you in the womb I knew you; before you were born I sanctified you; I ordained you a prophet to the nations."

There was a calling woven into the spiritual makeup of Jeremiah. He was to speak to nations and kings. He was to destroy and tear things down and plant and build things up. In the first chapter of his book, we get a glimpse into the activation of that calling. Each of us has a calling in our spiritual DNA too. It is who we are an atomic level. If you will submit to God in the littlest things, God will prepare you for your primary assignment. Did not Jesus say that if we were "faithful over a few things [He would] make us ruler over many things" (Matt. 25:23)? Scratch that itch and one day the power of your destiny will be unleashed.

Swedish researcher, David Ingvar, coined the phrase *memories of the future*. He says the human brain creates patterns for future activity simply by envisioning it beforehand. His peer-reviewed published studies have shown that the synapsis firing when one is daydreaming are pretty much the same synapsis firing when one is actually doing what one was daydreaming about. In other words, you and I are hardwired to dream, to envision the future. New Age visualization concepts and techniques are just twisted versions of a God-created mechanism by which His will can be accomplished in our lives. It is possible for you, in advance, to see yourself being who God has called you to be, doing what God called you to do, to such an extent that when you are actually living the dream, it feels like déjà vu. You are actually remembering the future.

In his classic, *Confessions*, Saint Augustine observes,

> Expectation refers to the future, and memory to the past. On the other hand, the tension in an act belongs to the present: through it the future is transformed into the past. Hence an act may contain something that refers to what has not yet come to pass.

Faith in the present always connects us to the past and to the future. God spoke the Word in the past. It will come to pass in the future, but in the present, we are connected to both the past and the future. As the church, when we take communion, we are in the present, but we are also connected to the past and the future by remembering the Lord's death and anticipating His return (see 1 Corinthians 11:23–26 and Luke 22:18). Psalm 22 is the psalm of the crucified Savior. Some scholars say Jesus quoted the entire psalm while on the cross. Psalm 24 is the psalm of the glorified Savior. It speaks of Him entering into His glory. But the twenty-third Psalm is the psalm of the ever-present Savior. Today, the Lord is my Shepherd. But His presence as my Shepherd is connected to His past as my crucified Lord and to His future reign as the glorified King of Kings. Let the reality of what He has done for you and called you to be become so big in you that as it manifests in your day-to-day life, it is already familiar territory; you are simply remembering the future.

Vision Demands Discipline

*If you don't have a vision for your body,
you'll eat anything (no restraints).
If you don't have a vision for your finances,
you'll spend it all (no restraints).
If you don't have a vision for your life,
you'll do anything (no restraints).*
—Terry Savelle Foy

When I was a kid, a preacher and his family visited my church. They were church planters, or *home missionaries*, as my tribe called them in those days. They were travelling and raising support for their work in the western part of the United States. This family left a lasting impression on my not yet fully developed frontal lobe. First, they looked miserable. Seriously, they looked broken, depressed, defeated, and demoralized. Second, and I know this is shallow, but they looked homely, out of style and out of touch. When the guy got up to preach, all my suspicions were confirmed. I made a decision that day. "I will *never* do what this guy does! It's too dangerous! Look at him! Not only does it kill your joy, it kills your cool factor, your moxie, your mojo! I will *never* be a church planter!"

I do not know what happened to that guy and his family. I hope they succeeded beyond their wildest dreams and fulfilled the call of God on their lives. But for me, never say never. Little did I know, I would, indeed, do what they did—plant churches. Hopefully, I have done so with a different disposition, although at times, I have certainly felt like they looked! But when I saw that family all those years ago, I was *already* in process. God had already called me, wired me, programmed me in such a way, that I would never find fulfillment until, and unless, I stepped into the risky enterprise of church planting. It was part of my spiritual DNA. It was who I was at my core, even though I had yet to discover this reality.

Ironically, church planting has been the lion's share of my calling. In over thirty years of ministry, I have never served as lead pastor of a church that I did not plant. All of my life, God had been preparing me to plant churches although I was blind to it at the beginning. I did not see myself as having the charisma or chutzpa to do something as audacious as church planting. The level of confrontation and sacrifice required seemed overwhelming to me, as well as, the insurmountable odds and financial hardships. Had you asked me: "Do you have what it takes to plant a church?" My answer would have been an emphatic, "No!" But through the years, Valerie and I *have* planted two churches, oversaw the planting of a third, and we may plant more. And in case you are wondering, Valerie felt the same way I did about church planting. She did not see it as part of her future either. But somewhere down the line, we *did* catch a glimpse; we *did* start seeing ourselves as church planters. We certainly understood it to be a daunting task, unachievable on our own, but still we saw ourselves succeeding with God's help. Like Paul, we started to believe we could do all He called us to do through Christ who gives us strength (see Philip. 4:13).

The truth is, Valerie and I have never been able to do for God what we *have done*. Let that sink in. We have always reached beyond our own abilities and attempted to do things that we could not do because we knew He had called us to do those things. Through the years, we have seen mountains move, and we have walked on water, as it were. Of course, it was not us alone. God strengthened and enabled us. But I would add, it was not God alone either. This is an important point: In His redemptive plans and purposes, *we* had a part to play and *He* had a part to play. We have learned to flow in a vibrant partnership with the author and finisher of our faith (Heb. 12:22). Also, it is important to note that there were people who partnered with us as well. God connected us to them. Perhaps I should say, God connected them to the dream He had placed in us, and they were inspired to help us in prayer, finances, and encouragement. Ultimately, we were all partnering with God. When you partner with God, He will connect you to the people He has foreordained to help you fulfill your dream.

God wants to partner with you. He has called you to do something you *cannot* do without His help, and it is something He *will* not do without your help. You may be thinking, *That's outrageous! He doesn't need us! He can do anything!* When David Livingstone was pursuing his God-dream to bring Jesus to Africa, he applied for financial assistance to a missionary society in Scotland. After considering his request, the leaders of the missionary society told him, "Young man, when God sees fit to evangelize Africa, He will do it without your help." That is not the way it works.

Of course, God can do anything He wants, but in His sovereignty, He has designated a role for us to play in His plan. For instance, He does not preach the Gospel. He has left that task to us. He no longer lays His hands on the sick, we do. The fact is, because of our union with Him by way of the Blood of the New Covenant, He *is* preaching and laying hands on the sick, but it is *through us*. We are His body, and as the Body of Christ, He is using our voice and our hands, our gifts, and our talents (see Romans 12:5, 1 Corinthians 12:12–27, Ephesians 3:6 and 4:15–16, Colossians 1:18, 24). The reality is, Christ is living through us (Gal. 2:20). Jesus will not plant a church, start a business, get a degree, or do anything else that He has called us to do. We must discover those callings and begin to see ourselves fulfilling them. As we are faithful to do so, to plant and water, as it were, He is faithful to bless our efforts and give the increase (see 1 Corinthians 3:6). A passerby noticed a farmer's field that was filled with a ripened crop. He said to the farmer, "God sure has blessed your field." To which the farmer replied, "You should have seen it when God had it by Himself!" We are called to be co-laborers with the Lord.

Ask yourself again, "Who am I? What does God want me to do?" There is a calling on your life. As a believer in Jesus, God has filled you with glorious purpose, and there is supernatural power within you ready to be unleashed. Not only does God want you to catch a glimpse, but He wants you to become highly developed in the vision that He has for your life. But you must understand: vision will change the way you live.

The Narrow Gate

In the King James Version of the Bible, Proverbs 29:18 says, "Where there is no vision, the people perish." The New King James Version puts it like this, "Where there is no revelation, the people cast off restraint." When we have no vision or revelation of the true life God intends us to live, we "perish" because we have no restraints, no controls to channel us in the direction of our calling. A lake is a river that is not focused. It is stagnant and going nowhere. A river, however, is a lake that *is* focused. It has boundaries and restrictions, banks that channel it in one direction, making it powerful and deep, and it is on the move. It is going somewhere. Like a river, when we see who we are in Christ and what we are called to do, we must discipline ourselves to flow only in the direction of our calling.

Notice John 8:31 and 32: "Then Jesus said to those Jews who believed Him, 'If you abide in my word, you are my disciples indeed. And you shall know the truth, and the truth shall make you free.'" It takes discipline to abide in His word, but abiding in His word also *brings* discipline. As the truth of who we are in Christ is revealed to us, it is our responsibility to focus on that, to narrow our way of thinking and living. That is discipline. That is discipleship. Practically speaking, that means there are some things we can do and there are some things we cannot do, if we are to fulfill our destiny. Jesus spoke of this in Matthew 7:13 and 14:

> Enter by the narrow gate; for wide is the gate and broad is the way that leads to destruction, and there are many who go in by it. Because narrow is the gate and difficult is the way which leads to life, and there are few who find it.

To be the man or woman of God He has called you to be and to do what He has called you to do requires you to live a life governed by that high calling. You must live from the perspective of the new you. Second Corinthians 5:17

says, "Therefore, if anyone is in Christ, he is a new creation; old things have passed away; behold, all things have become new." The new you should control the old you. In other words, "the elder shall serve the younger" (see Genesis 25:23 and Romans 9:12). This principle is lined out over and over in the Bible. Cain served Abel. Esau served Jacob. Joseph's brothers were subordinate to him. The "old you" should be completely surrendered to the will of the "new you," and the "new you" should be completely surrendered to the will of the Father. As a matter of fact, the "old you" was crucified with Christ and Christ lives through the "new you" (see Galatians 2:20). First Corinthians 6:19 and 20 puts it like this:

> Or do you not know that your body is the temple of the Holy Spirit who is in you, whom you have from God, and you are not your own? For you were bought at a price; therefore glorify God in your body and in your spirit, which are God's.

"You are not your own" means you cannot live to like your old man lived. You must live to please the Spirit. Your life must be governed by the call of God on your life. You must live up to that high calling in the way you behave and think. You present your body and renew your mind (see Romans 12:1, 2). You believed in Jesus and you continue to walk in His word, which requires discipline and brings discipline.

When you get a vision of yourself as God sees you, your life narrows, which enables God to help you fulfill the vision. Over the years, Valerie and I have developed in this narrow life. His vision for us has governed our language, behavior, and choices and directed our steps along a narrow path. Had we not seen ourselves as God sees us and stayed true to that vision, our lives would certainly have been very different today. If you can see yourself as He sees you and let that vision *govern* you, you are destined to live an extraordinary life—not just life, but life more abundantly (John 10:10).

Pregnant with Destiny

I love Walt Disney World's Space Mountain roller coaster. I have ridden it many times. Every time I stand in that line, I see the same sign: "Expectant mothers should not ride." The reason why is because the thrill of the roller coaster has the ability to harm the baby and the mother. When you are pregnant with divine destiny, you cannot just live however you please. There are some things you can do—and there are some things you cannot do. Your life has to be regulated by what you are carrying. Your calling must be protected at all costs. Too many Christians live recklessly, putting their calling at risk. As you focus in on who you are in Christ, your path will narrow. Some options are off the table. You must respect the sanctity of what you are carrying inside of you. You are filled with life and potential. The vision inside of you was sired by the Holy Spirit and will ultimately glorify the Lord Jesus Christ. Make your choices accordingly, and rest assured, on God's side, He is protecting the vision in astounding ways.

When you are pregnant with destiny, God takes everything you encounter and orchestrates it into a grand and beautiful symphony. He weaves *all things* into the tapestry of your calling. Romans 8:28 says:

> And we know that all things work together for good to those who love God,

to those who are the called according to His purpose. For whom He foreknew, He also predestined to be conformed to the image of His Son, that He might be the firstborn among many brethren. Moreover whom He predestined, these He also called; whom He called, these He also justified; and whom He justified, these He also glorified.

If you love Jesus and walk in the calling He has predetermined for your life, He will cause everything to work *for* you, even if, at first, it seems to work against you. There is a pattern to which you must be conformed. That pattern restricts and limits us to be who He has called us to be. The calling is two-fold: to be like Him in resurrection power and future glory, but also to walk in our specific calling while here on earth. Both the infinite and the temporal aspects of our calling are imperative. If we do not have a vision as to how we are to conform to His image, calling, and purpose, then we will live any old way. But if we have a vision of our destiny, then we will live in such a way that His will for our lives becomes a reality in this flesh-and-blood, physical world, and in the world to come.

Composing Your I Am Statement

Throughout this book, I have suggested that you find what God has already said about you in the Bible, meditate on those scriptures, confess them daily, and discipline yourself to only speak in agreement with them. The nuances and specifics of who God says you are and what He has called you to do will emerge from there. I suggest that you physically look up the Bible references listed in chapter 5. Get yourself a "primary Bible" for daily reading and study. Make sure it is one you can write in. Start with the first reference from chapter 5, look it up, and write down any insights you may have in regards to that verse. I have an old Cambridge wide margin reference Bible, and I love to chase down the references within each verse as well. Then, I notate the next verse from my list, thus creating a chain of references that I can easily follow. Go through the referenced verses in different translations. Look up the Hebrew and the Greek (one study tool I like to use is blueletterbible.com). As you meditate on these verses, say them out loud, personalize them by inserting your name in them. They are speaking of you. They are telling you who you are.

In our I Am Statement, Valerie and I began with the basics. Notice: "I am a successful pastor of a powerful and growing church." I *am* a pastor. The story of how I knew I was called to be a preacher and pastor is found in Praying

Your I Am Statement in the Spirit and Vision Demands Discipline chapters. That awareness grew out of time spent in God's presence. You have to spend time in His presence, surrendering to His will. Once I discovered my calling, however, I began to realize that I am not just any pastor. I am a *successful* pastor. Why would I say that? Because the Word tells me that if I do not let the Word depart from my mouth but meditate on it day and night, that I would have good success (see Joshua 1:8). And the church where I serve is not just any church, it is a powerful and growing church. Why would I say that? Because the Word tells me that Jesus is building His church and that the gates of hell shall not prevail against it and that He adds to the church (see Matthew 16:18 and Acts 2:47).

Next, I confess: "I lead with wisdom, excellence, boldness, and confidence." Why would I say that? Because the Word tells me that if I lack wisdom, I should ask God for it and that He would grant it (see James 1:5). Joseph had a spirit of excellence in a lesser covenant, and I walk in excellence in this better covenant (see Genesis 41:38 and Hebrews 8:6). I have been made the righteousness of God and the righteous are bold as a lion, and He has not given me a spirit of fear but of power, love, and sound mind (see 2 Corinthians 5:21, Proverbs 28:1, 2 Timothy 1:7).

Next, I confess: "I am a man of tremendous influence. I have favor with God, favor with man, and I am feared in hell," Why would I say that? Because we have seen how faith-filled people of God are recognized in the spirit realm and the Word says "when a man's ways please the Lord, He causes even his enemies to be at peace with him" (see Acts 19:15 and Proverbs 16:7).

Then I confess: "I plant and water with joy and faith knowing God is giving the increase and I am anxious for nothing." What is the basis of me saying this? Because the Word says that some plant and others water, but God gives the increase, and the Word says "God loves a cheerful giver" and goes on to say "be anxious for nothing, but in everything by prayer and supplication, with thanksgiving, let your requests be made known to God" (see 1 Corinthians 3:6, 2 Corinthians 9:7, and Philippians 4:6).

When it comes to me being "a ridiculous giver known for my generosity," that is based on the aforementioned "cheerful giver" passage which includes a determination to be a giver, as led by the Holy Spirit (see 2 Corinthians 9:6–7). The "debts are being eliminated and reserves are being generated" aspect of our prayer is based on Deuteronomy 28:12 and Proverbs 22:7, which speak of God's people being the lender and not the borrower, and many other verses that say God will financially bless His people, including Malachi 3:11, which says God will "rebuke the devourer" for His people.

Now that you know the biblical foundation for our little prayer, you can build your own. Here is a template to get you started.

> I am a successful _____ of a powerful and growing _____.
> I lead with wisdom, excellence, boldness, and confidence.
> I am a man/woman of tremendous influence. I have favor with God, favor with man, and I am feared in hell.
> I plant and water with joy and faith knowing God is giving the increase and I am anxious for nothing.
> I am a ridiculous giver, known for my generosity, and I am a blessing to the Body of Christ worldwide.
> Debts are being eliminated, reserves are being generated, _____ is a financial power-

house with more than enough to do what God has called us to do.

People are looking at me and saying, "Of all people, I never thought it would be you who was so blessed."

Arrange this as you will. Make it personal. Change the wording to fit you. Base it on scripture and who God has called you to be and then pray it every day. It will build you up and fortify you to walk into the fullness of your calling.

In the introduction to this book, I mentioned my friend Greg and a question he asked his students in detention many years ago. I ask the same question to you: Who are you? Have you gotten a glimpse of who you really are? Do you have a vision for your life? Who does God say you are? What has He called you to do? I encourage you to spend time praying and asking God what His plans are for your life. Where do you fit into His redemptive scheme? I am convinced it is well worth your time to pursue the answer to these questions.

Speak what the written word of God has already declared about you and ask God to reveal to you His specific will for your life. What is your destiny and calling in the twenty-first century? As He begins to reveal to you His plan for your life, begin to put it into words, into a working statement, that you can pray over and over. This is your I Am Statement. Get into agreement with Him, and build that vision big inside you. Be relentless in your pursuit of it, and turn the world upside down for Jesus!

About the Author

Donavon is a church planter, preacher, teacher, worship leader, and singer-songwriter who has ministered throughout the United States and around the world. He is known as a visionary and innovator who constantly inspires others to attempt great things for God. He is an encourager who is known for saying, "What looks like the end of the road is just a bend in the road. Get up and move on." He has been married to Valerie for over thirty years, and together, they planted LifePoint Church in 2006, where he currently serves as lead pastor. He and Valerie are the parents of three, grandparents of four, and are residing in the Baton Rouge area.

CPSIA information can be obtained
at www.ICGtesting.com
Printed in the USA
LVHW101123070722
722843LV00011B/294